Called 2 Love
Like Jesus

A collection of
experiential devotions

BroadStreet
P U B L I S H I N G

D1294442

BroadStreet Publishing® Group, LLC
Savage, Minnesota, USA
BroadStreetPublishing.com

Called 2 Love Like Jesus

Contents

Week 5   Love in the Household of Faith

Week 6   Love on Mission

In the Upper Room
with Jesus

"A new commandment I give to you, that you love one another; as I have loved you, that you also love one another. By this all will know that you are My disciples, if you have love for one another."

JOHN 13:34–35 NKJV

Imagine the scene: The Savior sits quietly with his disciples in the upper room. The mood is somber; the feelings intense. The loyal followers know something is troubling the Teacher, but can't quite grasp the gravity of his words. Jesus turns to the men—and with a sense of tenderness and care, he tells the disciples that he will only be with them a little longer. Where Jesus is about to go, they cannot.

These words would have been earth-shattering to the disciples. They literally left everything to follow Jesus—and after three years together, they hear him say he plans to leave. The disciples sit up, lean in, and strain to hear what Jesus has to say next.

With tenderness still in his voice, Christ shares a fresh perspective. He gives a new commandment. We might be tempted to think that in these final moments, Jesus would emphasize certain things to do or particular behaviors to avoid. Instead, in these last moments with his disciples, Jesus gives a command—but it was a command to love. The command to love wasn't new, but the extent of love would be newly defined. The disciples had no idea *how* Jesus was about to redefine love, but they would soon come face to face with the one who is love. Love would be displayed on a cross and newly defined by Christ's example.

The calling and commandment of John 13:34 is not only for the followers in the upper room, it is a calling for each of us. The Savior is calling for there to be a special presence and experience of love among followers of Jesus. Christ is calling for love to be the identifying mark of his disciples. Love is to be at the heart of who we are and what we do.

Called 2 Love: Like Jesus has been written to support, challenge, and encourage you in how to respond to Christ's call to love. Why is our response to this call so important?

- Without a renewed focus on experiencing love from God and expressing love for God, our faith becomes only about doing things for God.

- Without a prioritization of love, marriages dissolve, families break down, and every relationship is marked by disconnection and aloneness.

- Without a fresh testimony of love and unity, Jesus-followers are more often labeled for their differences of doctrine or religious duty rather than for a heart of love for one another.

- Without consistent demonstrations of love, church ministry is irrelevant—and a world which desperately needs the hope of Jesus stops listening.

Therefore, *Called 2 Love: Like Jesus* is intended to help you prioritize your response to Christ's call to love. We invite you to allow the Lord to guide you into fresh experiences of his love for you and in turn, to voice your love back to him. We're asking the Lord to guide you into fresh challenges of how you might demonstrate his love for others—beginning with your spouse, children, and family. We pray you will allow God to empower your love for his church and to let there be a special renewed presence of unity among his people. And finally, may you sense God's fresh anointing as you share his love with others and live out his calling to love those who don't yet know the person of Jesus.

Introduction

Called 2 Love: Like Jesus is designed to bring a fresh perspective to what it means to love Jesus and people. The goal of this resource is to help you move beyond knowing and understanding God's command to love and move toward more experiences of that love. As you will see, when you deepen your experience of God's love, you will be better equipped to love your spouse, children, family, and friends. As you embrace more of God's love for you, you will be empowered to love other Jesus-followers and to ultimately express love as you live on mission for him.

This resource is all about relationships—fresh experiences of Christ's love for you and then a focus on the priority of loving others. This relational focus will require a relational faith—because it's only a relational faith that produces a prioritization of love.

In order to fully illustrate what a relational faith includes, we have defined forty different Spirit-empowered outcomes categorized into four themes (see appendices 2 and 3). Each Spirit-empowered outcome will be noted with the following symbol:

A Spirit-empowered disciple:

- **Loves the Lord** (L1-10): Here you will find specific times for expression of your love for Jesus.

- **Lives the Word** (W1-10): These moments will equip you in how to live out specific Scriptures from God's Word.

- **Loves People** (P1-10): You'll learn how to discern the relational needs of others and to share God's love in meaningful ways.

- **Lives his Mission** (M1-10): In these moments, you will plan to actively share Jesus' love with others and tell them about the one who lives inside of you.

Our world needs more people living as Spirit-empowered disciples who are making disciples who, in turn, make disciples. Thus, *Called 2 Love: Like Jesus* rightly focuses on the powerful simplicity of ...

- Receiving God's love for us and then loving him as our first priority.

- Living his Word—because there's power and possibility in experiencing Scripture.

- Loving people by developing a lifestyle of giving first; and taking initiative to love your spouse, children, friends, family, and members of the faith community.

- Living his mission—which means building a lasting legacy, as you share Jesus' hope with others.

As you read through this resource, we invite you to walk:

- In the light of God's Son—John 8:12

- In the light of God's Word—Psalm 119:105

- In the light of God's people—Matthew 5:14

As a means of encouragement, each day of this forty-day journey contains an excerpted article from a well-known author and moments for you to pause and walk in the light. It's only when we walk in the light of Jesus, his Word, and his people that we will see our lives change. That's why you will be invited to pause each day of the journey to:

- Encounter Jesus

- Experience Scripture

- Engage with your community

Finally, the Great Commandment Network is thrilled to serve each contributor and ministry partner through this resource. Our resource development and training team serves various partners as they work faithfully to equip others in a lifestyle of love. May Jesus richly bless the unity, commitment, and faith that *Called 2 Love: Like Jesus* represents.

Terri Snead
Executive Editor, Great Commandment Network

The Great Commandment Network is an international collaborative network of strategic kingdom leaders from the faith community, marketplace, education, and caregiving fields who prioritize the powerful simplicity of the words of Jesus to love God, love others, and see others become His followers (Matthew 22:37–40, Matthew 28:19–20).

Week 1

Why Love Like Jesus?

Ministry and life purpose flow out of a common center—first through our intimate relationship with Jesus and then through caring connections with spouse and family. Effective discipleship flows out of our closest, most connected relationships.

As a follower of Jesus, the important relationships with spouse, family, ministry, and mission are relationships to which only you can give careful attention. Maximum impact for God's Kingdom will first require our true commitment to loving like Jesus in these closest relationships.

As you consider your relationship with Jesus and the other key relationships of your life, think of them as ever expanding concentric circles that reflect the calling to love God has for every part of your life. These circles are based on our Lord's Great Commission and the Great Commandment. Since Great Commission living is empowered by Great Commandment love, the experience of our loving relationship with Jesus is the center point for love experienced in all other relationships.

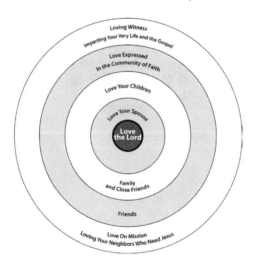

"'You must love the Lord your God with all your heart, all your soul, and all your mind.' This is the first and greatest commandment. A second is equally important: 'Love your neighbor as yourself.' The entire law and all the demands of the prophets are based on these two commandments."
MATTHEW 22:37–40

"Therefore, go and make disciples of all the nations, baptizing them in the name of the Father and the Son and the Holy Spirit. Teach these new disciples to obey all the commands I have given you. And be sure of this: I am with you always, even to the end of the age."

MATTHEW 28:19–20

It's His Command

Jesus left exact instructions about how the world was to know about him. He intended for the love that his followers have for him to be demonstrated in practical and observable love for others. In other words, the world would come to believe in the love of God as his people truly demonstrate love for one another.

Scripture says it best: "'So now I am giving you a new commandment: Love each other. Just as I have loved you, you should love each other. Your love for one another will prove to the world that you are my disciples'" (John 13:34–35).

From "Love One Another"
by Ronnie Floyd

It's both exciting and equally convicting to prioritize loving one another as the theme for our day. Here are four, living illustrations why this is a fantastic and needed theme.

Illustration #1: "Love one another" are the words of Jesus in John 13:34, "Love one another. Just as I have loved you." I was reminded while reading through Psalm 119 from the New Living Translation of these words found in verse 37: "Turn my eyes from worthless things and give me life through your word." We need the priority of loving one another because nothing leads to life more than the Bible, the Word of God. Our lives are filled with so many worthless things, but these words of Jesus are words of life.

Illustration #2: The condition of churches in America today remind us of the need to re-prioritize loving one another. Over eighty percent of the churches in America are plateaued or declining. Most of the time this occurs due to the lack of health within the church. Most often, it is because "love one another" is not being practiced within the church. In fact, many times, there is great unrest and a lack of true Christian fellowship among believers in these churches.

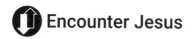 **Encounter Jesus**

But the student who is fully trained
will become like the teacher.
LUKE 6:40

In order to become Christ-followers who truly love one another, we must spend more time with the God of love. Therefore, take the next few moments and imagine Jesus is standing before you. He's the Teacher of love and the One who IS love. Imagine that Christ makes this gentle but passionate invitation personally to you: "I want you to become like me and learn from me, so you can share my love with others. I'm calling you to be a student of my love, but this calling comes with a promise. I am ready to show you love in such incredible ways that my love spills over onto others. Learning from me, means soaking in my love for you!" Now voice your personal prayer back to Jesus.

Jesus, I accept your invitation. I want to learn from you. I want to experience your love in new and meaningful ways so that I am equipped to _____.

Illustration #3: We need to refocus on our call to love one another because our relationships are in serious trouble. Marriages and families are falling apart across our country and our world. 1 Corinthians 13:8 says "Love never ends." This kind of enduring, lasting love is missing in so many friendships, marriages and families. Therefore, "Love one another" is a message that is absolutely needed for our day. A focus on loving one another is needed across all relationships, including our workplaces, communities, and cities.

Illustration #4: Finally, the "love one another" theme is right for our day because our government's talking points and contentious efforts rarely lead our country to love. Negative words spoken about one another lead to ongoing actions that are preventing our country from moving forward. Vitriolic speech and divisive actions serve as living testimonies of how much America needs the message of "love one another". None of this is right. We can differ with other people, and yet, remain true to our calling to love.

The Church must lead the way to love. An unloving and divided church cannot call an unloving and divided nation to love and unity. Yes, the church must lead the way: Love one another!

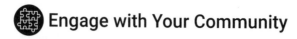 Engage with Your Community

My faithfulness and unfailing love will be with him,
and by my authority he will grow in power.
PSALM 89:24

Leading the way in loving others, begins with loving those nearest to us. Think about the person in your life who needs to experience the love of Jesus most. God is calling you to love them like Jesus. He's also committed to being with you in the journey and empower you in loving well. Claim his promise and then share your love-like-Jesus desire with your spouse, friend or small group.

Lord, I know you want me to love _____ like you love him/her. I need to learn from you because ...

I am claiming your promise of faithfulness and love that never fails. Because of your love and faithfulness, I can grow in my power and ability to _____.

 Experience Scripture

We loved you so much that we shared with you
not only God's Good News but our own lives, too.
1 Thessalonians 2:8

Reflect again on this person who most needs to experience Jesus' love. How might you share your life with this person, so they experience more of Christ's love? Does this person need your support, acceptance, forgiveness, compassion, humility, kindness, encouragement or hope? Plan your practical demonstration of Christ's love here.

I sense that my _____ (spouse, child, friend, neighbor, co-worker or family member) needs more of Jesus' love. I think he/she most needs me to give _____. I plan to demonstrate that love by _____.

 P3. A Spirit-empowered disciple consistently discerns the relational needs of others and shares God's love in meaningful ways.

It's Our Grateful Response to His Grace

For this is how much God loved the world—he gave his one and only, unique Son as a gift. So now everyone who believes in him will never perish but experience everlasting life. (John 3:16)

The most familiar verse in the entire Bible is about a God who loves. It's startling when we begin to imagine the depth of just how much God loves; it's startling to imagine the miracle of Jesus!

Throughout the pages of Scripture, we read Christ's divinely inspired words and get a glimpse of his amazing miracles. Yet through all these revolutionary moments, we don't want to miss this: Everything Jesus said and did was meant to call attention to how he loved. Take a moment to reflect on just a few of the startling ways that Jesus loves:

- Jesus startled lepers with loving compassion. He healed their bodies and brought dignity to their lives. Sometimes Christ even touched the lepers himself, to bring about healing (Luke 5:12–13; 17:11–19).

- Jesus startled a Samaritan woman when he broke all cultural conventions by asking her for a drink of water (John 4:4–26). In the midst of her shame and rejection, the Savior entrusted her with a conversation about eternal things and extended a message of mercy and justice (Micah 6:8).

- Jesus startled the woman caught in adultery when he knelt beside her, joined her at the point of her pain, and extended hope and forgiveness. Christ dispersed the accusers and then offered restoration. He extended grace, as well as a loving challenge: "'Go now and leave your life of sin'" (John 8:10–11).

 **Encounter Jesus**

Give thanks to the Lord, for he is good! His faithful love endures forever.
PSALM 136:1

Now, pause to remember some of the startling ways that Jesus has loved you. Reflect, remember, and then give him thanks:

Jesus, you first startled me with love when you brought me into relationship with you. I'm so grateful that I have relationship with you because _____.

Jesus, today I am amazed at the love and grace you have shown me, especially as you _____.

From *Love Like That*
by Les Parrott

You can't study the life of Jesus and avoid life-altering grace. He is the personification of grace. He acknowledges the ugliness of sin but chooses to see beyond it. In each of the four Gospels, Jesus radiates grace not only in his teachings, but in his life—toward a woman caught in adultery; a Roman soldier; a Samaritan woman with serial husbands; a shame-filled prostitute. Grace runs rampant in the life of Jesus. "Jesus did not identify the person with his sin," wrote theologian Helmut Thielicke, "but rather saw in this sin something alien, something that really did not belong to him, something … from which he would free him and bring him back to his real self."

Nowhere did Jesus more clearly separate the sin from the sinner than in the last moments of his earthly life. After unspeakable and heartless torture, Roman soldiers take Jesus the Nazarene a short distance from Jerusalem's city wall to a place the locals named Golgotha, or "Place of the Skull." They initiate the barbaric ritual of nailing him to a cross. Typically, they begin by giving the victim a mild painkiller—not as an act of mercy, but to make it easier for them to nail his limbs to the wooden beams. Jesus refuses the medicine, probably to remain lucid.

Two soldiers put all their weight on his extended arms as another drives six-inch iron nails through each hand. His feet are flexed at an extreme angle, lapped one over the other and nailed into place. They lift the cross up, guiding the base into a hole in the ground with a jarring thud. As the ruthless death squad steadies the cross to keep it upright, Jesus—who has hardly spoken in hours—whispers a prayer: "Father, forgive them, for they do not know what they're doing."

Grace beyond measure. Not only was Jesus suffering physically from this torment, he was the object of taunts and verbal abuse from the Roman killers and onlookers: "Ha! You who are going to destroy the temple and rebuild it in three days, save yourself, and come down from the cross!" The religious leaders mocked him too: "He saved others, but he cannot save himself." Enduring unimaginable suffering, the Nazarene offers grace and forgiveness to his persecutors.

But his grace-giving doesn't stop there. Jesus, thirty-three years old, hanging a few feet above the earth between two robbers, minutes before his death, has one more act of grace to give.

One of the criminals hurls insults at Jesus: "Aren't you the Messiah? Save yourself and us!"

But the other felon rebukes his fellow crook: "We are punished justly, for we are getting what our deeds deserve. But this man has done nothing wrong." Then this robber adds: "Jesus, remember me when you enter your kingdom."

Jesus responds to him, "Don't worry; I will. Today you will join me in paradise."

Jesus could have rained down condemnation. He could have condemned his coldhearted death squad as well as the sanctimonious leaders and this convicted criminal on a cross next to him. He could have prayed for God to strike them all down. But Jesus—the man of unconditional acceptance—even in his last breaths gives grace!

 Experience Scripture

We are therefore Christ's ambassadors,
as though God were making his appeal through us.
2 CORINTHIANS 5:20

Reflect again on the grace and love that you have received from Jesus. Next, think about the people whom God regularly places in your life. You have been placed there as his ambassador. Jesus wants to extend his love and acceptance through you. He wants to communicate his support, forgiveness, and hope through you to others. As Christ's ambassador, ask the Holy Spirit to make 2 Corinthians 5:20 real for you because of your gratitude for his grace.

Who among your family, friends, coworkers, and acquaintances could benefit from:

• His forgiveness through you (no matter what their sin)?

• His acceptance through you (even before they change)?

• His support through you (even if they have not asked)?

 **Engage with Your Community**

I will tell everyone about the wonderful things you do.
PSALM 73:28

Tell a friend, spouse, or small group about your commitment to love like Jesus. Share about your desire to be Christ's ambassador—loving people like you have been loved by him.

I want to love _____ (share the name) like Jesus has loved me.

I plan to do that by _____.

 M2. A Spirit-empowered disciple selflessly demonstrates the love of Jesus with those in need of hope and justice—sharing God's compassion and forgiveness.

It's a Reflection of Our Identity

Loving like Jesus will require steady looks in the mirror. In order to live out our call, we must see ourselves the way Jesus sees us—nothing less and nothing more. In order to love others like Jesus loves, we must first be secure in our own identity. We must be confident in whose reflection is staring back at us in the mirror.

When you glance in the mirror, are you afraid you'll see "the one who's messed up" or the "one who'll never change"? If you're a child of God, when you look in the mirror, the person staring back at you is the "Beloved of God." That's who you are. The Creator made you, died for you, and declared that you are worth the gift of his Son. Only when you securely embrace that you are the "one who Jesus loves" will you be ready to love others like he does. So go ahead. Look. Discover who you really are. You'll like what you see!

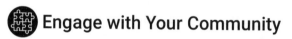 **Engage with Your Community**

to the praise of the glory of His grace,
which He freely bestowed on us in the Beloved.
EPHESIANS 1:6 NASB

Pause for a few moments. Plan out your response and schedule a time to talk to your spouse, friend, or small group. Share your response below:

God says that I am the "beloved of God." That is truth. That's who he says I am.

I embrace that truth most easily when _____.

I struggle to embrace that truth when _____.

From *Wild Goose Chase*

by Mark Batterson

Every summer I take a six-week preaching sabbatical. The reason is simple. It is so easy to get focused on what God wants to do through me that I totally neglect what God wants to do in me. So, I take off my sandals for six weeks. I go on vacation. I go to church with my family. And for several weeks during the summer, I just sit with our congregation, taking notes and singing songs like everyone else. My sabbatical is one way I keep the routine from becoming routine. But it's about more than just taking off my sandals. Let me explain.

Shortly after telling Moses to take off his sandals, God gave Moses one more curious command. He told Moses to throw down his staff.

> Then the LORD said to him, "What is that in your hand?" "A staff," he replied.
> The LORD said, "Throw it on the ground." Moses threw it on the ground
> and it became a snake, and he ran from it. Then the LORD said to him,
> "Reach out your hand and take it by the tail." So Moses reached out and
> took hold of the snake and it turned back into a staff in his hand. "This,"
> said the LORD, "is so that they may believe that the LORD, the God of their
> fathers—the God of Abraham, the God of Isaac and the God of Jacob—has
> appeared to you." (Exodus 4:2–5)

A shepherd's staff was a six-foot-long wooden rod that was curved at one end. It functioned as a walking stick, a weapon, and a prod used to guide the flock. Moses never left home without his staff. That staff symbolized his security. It offered him physical security from wild animals. It provided his financial security—his sheep were his financial portfolio. And it was a form of relational security. After all, Moses worked for his father-in-law.

But the staff was more than just a form of security. It was also part of his identity. When Moses looked in the mirror, he saw a shepherd—nothing more; nothing less. And I think that's why Moses asked God to send someone else: "'Who am I, that I should go to Pharaoh and bring the Israelites out of Egypt?'" (Exodus 3:11). I love the way God answers his question by changing the focus. God says: "'I will be with you'" (Exodus 3:12). That doesn't really seem like an answer to Moses' question, does it? But I think it was God's way of saying, "Who you are isn't the issue; the issue is whose you are!"

Has God ever called you to throw something down? Something in which you find your security or put your identity? It's awfully hard to let go, isn't it? It feels like you are jeopardizing your future. And it feels like you could lose what is most important to you. But that is when you discover who you really are.

I agonize with you because I know how tough it is to throw down a staff. It was so hard to throw down my scholarship at the University of Chicago. It was so hard to leave the security of friends and family and move from Chicago to Washington, DC. But the only way you discover a new identity is by letting an old one go. And the only way you'll find your security in Christ is by throwing down the human securities we tend to cling to.

There is a branch of history called counterfactual theory that asks the what-if questions. So here's my counterfactual question: What if Moses had held on to his staff? I think the answer is simple: The shepherd's staff would have remained a shepherd's staff. I don't think God would have used Moses to deliver Israel. I think Moses would have gone right back to shepherding his flock.

If you aren't willing to throw down your staff, you forfeit the miracle that is at your fingertips. You must be willing to let go of an old identity in order to take on a new identity. And that is what happens to Moses. This is a miracle of transformation. Not just the staff turning into a snake, but a shepherd of sheep turning into the leader of a nation. But Moses had to throw down the shepherd's staff for it to be transformed into the rod of God.

As far as we know, this is the first miracle Moses ever experienced. If Moses had held on to the staff, he would have forfeited all those miracles. He would have spent the rest of his life counting sheep.

Where do you find your identity? What is the source of your security? Is it a title? A paycheck? A relationship? A degree? A name? There is nothing wrong with any of those things—as long as you can throw them down [for Christ].

If you find your security outside of Christ, you have a false sense of security. And you have a false sense of identity. As long as you hold onto your staff, you'll never know what you could have accomplished with God's help. And let me remind you of this: Your success isn't contingent upon what's in your hand. Your success is contingent upon whether God extends his mighty hand on your behalf. Therefore, let me issue a challenge. Throw down your staff and discover the adventure on the far side of routine.

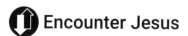 ## Encounter Jesus

This is real love—not that we loved God, but that he loved us
and sent his Son as a sacrifice to take away our sins.
1 JOHN 4:10

Jesus' sacrifice on the cross serves as a declaration of our worth in God's eyes. Imagine that Jesus is speaking to you from heaven. Listen to the words that are just for you: "You are especially valuable to me. You are important to me—so important that I laid down my life for you. I saw that you were in danger of being separated from me for all of eternity, so I acted. I rescued you because I love you and couldn't bear the thought of heaven without you. That's how I see you: one who is worth my sacrifice. You are my beloved one."

Now respond to Jesus' words:

Jesus, when I hear your declaration of my worth to you, I feel _____. Thank you for reminding me of the truth that my worth and my identity can only be declared by the one who created me and died for me.

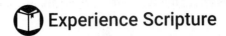 **Experience Scripture**

In reference to your former manner of life, lay aside the old self.
EPHESIANS 4:22

Ask God to reveal the "staff" that you need to throw down:

Lord, do I need to throw down …

• *A source of security or provision that's other than you?*

• *A label that I give myself or identity that's other than what you have declared?*

• *A habit or behavior that's contrary to your plan for my life?*

- *Some plans or decisions about my future that I have made apart from you?*

Lord, show me what I need to lay aside. Reveal it to me and then show me what you want for my life.

 L5. A Spirit-empowered disciple quickly acknowledges sins; asks for and receives forgiveness; and lives with a deep desire to always please Jesus.

It's Our Calling

From the "Called 2 Love Sermon Series"

by Great Commandment Network

A new command I give to you, that you love one another:
just as I have loved you, you also are to love one another.
JOHN 13:34 ESV

Think about the words of John 13:34 for a minute. They reveal the answers to some of life's most important questions. These words help you know how to answer the following:

- *Who is God?*

- *Who am I?*

- *What's my life's purpose?*

As we become more able to answer these three big questions in life, we'll gain clarity about who we are, who God is, and why we're on the planet! Let's look at how John 13:34 can be our guide.

1. Who Is He?

Notice the words of John 13:34 one more time. They're a command:

*"**A new command I give to you**, that you love one another: just as I have loved you, you also are to love one another"*
JOHN 13:34 ESV

Consider this:

- Who is the one person who gets to issue commands?

- Is it the Old Testament prophets? No.

- How about the New Testament Pharisees? No.

The New Testament Pharisees could declare edicts and laws, but never commands. To do so would have been to claim to be Jehovah. It is *Jesus*—the one who *is* God—who gave us this new command. The same God who gave the first Ten Commandments to Moses gave us an eleventh commandment: To love one another, as he has loved us.

Just as God has commanded us not to steal, murder, or covet (because he wants the best for our lives), he also commands us to love (Deuteronomy 10:12–13). In fact, the one commandment God gives extra clarity to and emphasis upon is his directive to love. Apparently God, who is the Creator of all things, the one in charge of all things and the one who sets the priority of all things, considers love to be at the top of the list. He is insistent that we get the importance of love. John 13:34 tells us that God, who is the ultimate authority, has called us to love!

> *"A new command I give to you,* **that you love one another:**
> **just as I have loved you**, *you also are to love one another"*
> JOHN 13:34 ESV

You may be asking yourself: "How am I going to be able to live out this command? I get that it's important, but I'm not exactly sure how to pull it off."

The key to living out God's command can also be found in John 13:34: "'Just as I have loved you.'" The key to living out God's command to love others is to experience more and more of his love for us. Take some time to do that now.

 Experience Scripture

> *Because your lovingkindness is better than life, my lips will praise you.*
> PSALM 63:3

Reflect on some of the significant moments of your life and remember the times when you sensed God's love—just for you. When did he provide for you? Protect you? Comfort you? Encourage you?

Praise the Lord out loud as your heart is moved with gratefulness:

God, I remember feeling especially loved by you when _____. I praise you because you are _____.

2. Who Are You?

This is the second of three big questions of life. Reflect again on the words of John 13:34:

> "A new command I give to you, that you love one another:
> **just as I have loved you**, you also are to love one another"
> JOHN 13:34 ESV

You might not yet fully believe it or feel it—but with these few words, "'Just as I have loved you,'" Jesus declared that *you* are the *beloved* of *God*!

If you have chosen to follow Jesus and accepted his gift of grace, you have had the privilege of being born again.

- Why did Christ sacrifice himself on the cross?

- Even more personally: For whom did he suffer and die?

- Who benefits from Jesus' death and resurrection?

Here's the truth that's reinforced in John 13:34: If Christ did not need to die for any other person in the whole world, he would have died for you—and he did! Allow yourself a moment to respond to this glorious truth. Jesus sacrificed himself in death and then was raised for you—for *you*. *You* are the beloved of God.

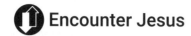 Encounter Jesus

Imagine Jesus giving himself just for you!

But God demonstrates His own love toward us,
in that while we were yet sinners, Christ died for us.
ROMANS 5:8

Begin to pray. As you do, listen to the Holy Spirit whisper to your heart, "He did it for you. He did it for you!"

Meditate on this thought: *"He did it for me."* Is your heart moved with gratitude, humility, or joy? Allow yourself a moment to respond to this glorious truth: Jesus sacrificed himself in death and then was raised for you.

You did it for me! Jesus, I am so grateful that you _____ because _____.

3. Why Are You Here?

The third and final question we must ask ourselves is: *Why am I here?*

"A new command I give to you, that you love one another:
*just as I have loved you, **you also are to love one another**."*
JOHN 13:34 ESV

This same passage of Scripture not only tells us who Jesus is and who we are, it also brings clarity to our life's purpose. With these few words, Christ declares that life's highest calling, most important goal, and most foundational purpose is to *love.*

With the words "'love one another,'" Jesus declares a purpose for his people. We are called to love!

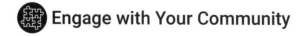 Engage with Your Community

And may the Lord make your love for one another and for all people grow and overflow, just as
our love for you overflows.
1 THESSALONIANS 3:12

Take a moment now and ask the Lord to reveal to you any way in which your spouse, child, friend, family member, co-worker, or neighbor might need to be loved. Is this person going through something painful, frustrating, overwhelming, or disappointing? Perhaps they are struggling in a relationship or have experienced a loss. Have there been challenges at work, at school, or at home with parents or siblings?

Plan to live out your call to love by meeting a practical need for this person. How could you give your time to demonstrate love? How might you share one of your talents in order to demonstrate love? How could you give a gift of money or resources to show love? Love this person like Jesus and demonstrate the reason why you are here! Complete the following and share your response with a spouse, friend, or small group.

I plan to live out my call to love by giving _____.

 M7. A Spirit-empowered disciple looks for opportunities to share time, gifts, talents, and money to fulfill and further the mission of Jesus

It's Our Legacy

Here's some good news for you, child of God! The Father has chosen you to be a part of his family. As a part of his family and as a recipient of God's grace, you are called to proclaim the Good News of Jesus. Galatians 1:15 reminds us: "But even before I was born, God chose me [you] and called me [you] by his marvelous grace. Then it pleased him to reveal his Son to me [you] so that I [you] would proclaim the Good News about Jesus."

 **Experience Scripture**

God chose you and called you by his marvelous grace.
GALATIANS 1:15

"Those who are with Him are called, chosen, and faithful."
REVELATION 17:14

   Would you take a moment to express your gratitude to God and voice your willingness to accept his calling? Say a prayer that includes these words:

God, I am so grateful that you chose me and called me to be a part of your family. I'm thankful that you revealed Jesus to me because ...

Because I am grateful to you, I accept your calling to proclaim Jesus and love like he loves. I especially want to love _____.

From *Parenting with Intimacy*

by Terri Snead

It sounds counterintuitive, but parents who are serious about living out their calling as disciple-makers must selflessly take care of themselves. Think about the flight attendant's instructions that are given to every parent traveling with small children: "If the cabin should lose pressure, your oxygen mask will drop from the ceiling. Be sure to put on your own mask before attending to your child." The same principle holds true in disciple-making. If you want to pass along God's love, grace, and compassion to your kids, you must experience these first yourself. If you want to impart a faith that's vibrant, relevant, and meaningful, pursue that kind of faith on your own. Make faith a priority—and then out of gratitude for God's work in your own life, share the same with others, especially your kids.

As you focus on taking care of yourself, if you're married, be sure to make it a priority to keep your marriage strong. As your child sees the strength of your marriage relationship, it gives him or her the freedom to grow, mature, and embrace a relationship with Jesus. If Mom and Dad's marriage is strong—not perfect, but strong—that gives the child permission to do the job that God has given them to do: to grow spiritually, emotionally, and physically. And remember: No matter what your marital status, God has not called you to be a perfect parent with perfect kids. He has called you to be a faithful parent, equipping your children to become all they can be in him.

Here's a next step in your pursuit of a vibrant, personal faith. A divine perspective is critical to our missional role because effective disciple-makers are always careful to affirm another's identity. As those who are called to love like Jesus, it's our job to intentionally confirm the identity that God has declared to be truth about his people. Affirming a person's identity means understanding who God has created them to be and what the Scriptures say about who they are in God's eyes. Scripture teaches three essential truths that will lead us to embrace an accurate view of how God sees us.

- **I am created in God's image.** A child (and every human being) needs our confirmation that they are a special creation, made in the likeness of God. They need to hear it from our lips and see it in our actions.

- **I am fallen but not worthless.** A child (and every human being) needs constant reminders that (just like their moms and dads), they are fallen and sinful, but they are also worth the gift of God's Son. Our works are worthless; we are not.

- **I am supremely and sacrificially loved.** A child (and every human being) needs affirmation of how much they are loved and to what lengths God was willing to go in order to show them he cares. God has entrusted you with his precious "gifts." Let him remind you to cherish them.

As parents help their child navigate this busy, craze[d]-filled world, we must be careful not to miss some of the real secrets of how to be a successful disciple-maker. Don't let *good things* distract you from the *best things*.

George Mueller, a nineteenth-century minister and author, was asked about his secrets for success. He answered, "As I look back on my life, what I see is that I was constantly brought to crossroads in my life—crossroads which demanded a choice of which way I should go. As I was brought to those crossroads, I believe the key to my success is that I seemed to have consistently chosen the least traveled path."

There's a broad road for parenting. It's a wide path where many travel. Let's be sure to model a vibrant faith of our own so that we're equipped to affirm a child's God-given identity and then launch them onto the road least traveled.

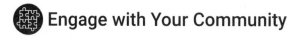 Engage with Your Community

I will tell about your righteous deeds all day long.
PSALM 71:24

An important aspect of loving like Jesus includes spiritual conversations. First, plan to have a spiritual conversation with your spouse, child, or friend. Talk to them about Jesus and how he is making a difference in your relationships. Your words might begin with these:

With your spouse:

> *Jesus has called me to love you like he loves you. How am I doing? Could you tell me one of the ways I'm loving you well and one of the ways you'd like to see me grow?*

With a child:

> *Jesus has given me the incredible job of being your mom/dad. I take that job seriously, and so Jesus has been helping me ...*

With a friend:

> *I have a new perspective on my relationships. Instead of just trying to get along with people, I'm trying to see them with the eyes of Jesus. It's making a huge difference in ...*

Look for ways to see people with the eyes of Jesus. Give them your undivided attention. Look for ways to hear with the ears of Jesus. Listen to their words and the needs behind them. Listen with a desire to know others more deeply.

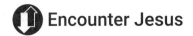 Encounter Jesus

Whatever is good and perfect is a gift coming down to us from God our Father,
who created all the lights in the heavens.
JAMES 1:17 NLT

Pause and imagine yourself standing before your spouse, friends, or children— your gifts from the Lord. Each gift is uniquely packaged, preciously wrapped, and carefully presented.

As you admire your beautifully wrapped gifts, you look over your shoulder to see Jesus standing next to you. Jesus leans forward to look more closely at the people you love, and seems to gaze in awe of his creation. He smiles with satisfaction and approval. His eyes sparkle as he admires every aspect of these precious gifts. Speaking with admiration, the Master Creator reminds you of how he knows each person intimately; he formed them in the womb (Jeremiah 1:5). Jesus reminds you that he notices each part of their day—when they rise up and when they lie down (Psalm 139:1–3). Christ lovingly recalls how he knows and admires each person's gifts and talents (Psalm 139:14–16). Jesus offers reassurance that he hears each person's thoughts and intentions and knows the intricacies of their character (Psalm 139:23). Jesus leaves your side—but before he does, he whispers an invitation: *Will you join me? Let's work together to unwrap these gifts. Will you join me in knowing these loved ones so intimately that we can admire how special they are together?*

Voice your prayer to Jesus. Tell him that you want to have the Creator's perspective:

Jesus, when I look at the special people in my life, I want to see what you see. Give me your eyes to see their unique beauty. Give me your ears to hear their needs. Give me your heart of approval for them. I want to join you in loving them well.

 P4. A Spirit-empowered disciple sees people as Jesus sees them. Jesus sees people as needing both a relationship with God (and his forgiveness) as well as a relationship with others.

It's Others' Hope

The Great Commission of making disciples gives us our destination, while the Great Commandment of loving the Lord and loving others provides the road map to get there. As we become great lovers of God and lovers of people, that "becoming" will draw others to Jesus. Becoming is the critical ingredient, the one we don't want to omit in our spiritual journey. But it is also the ingredient that is easiest to lose sight of; the one that is often neglected without thinking about it. Loving like Jesus is first about becoming. Then, as we become great lovers of God and lovers of people, we will live a life that reflects the life of Christ.

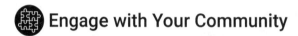 Engage with Your Community

Imitate God, therefore, in everything you do,
because you are his dear children. Live a life filled with love.
EPHESIANS 5:1–2

Stop right now and pray the prayer below or pray later with a spouse, friend, or small group. Ask God to help you become an even better expression of his love—so that more and more people will be drawn to Jesus:

Lord, I come to you because I don't want to forget or omit the necessity of becoming more like you. Make me more like Jesus so that others can see you and be drawn to you.

From *The Great Omission*

by Dallas Willard

When Jesus walked among humankind there was a certain simplicity to being his disciple. Primarily it meant to go with him, in an attitude of observation, study, obedience, and imitation. There were no correspondence courses. One knew what to do and what it would cost. Simon Peter [said], "'Look, we have left everything and followed you'" (Mark 10:28). Family and occupations were deserted for long periods to go with Jesus as he walked from place to place announcing, showing, and explaining the here-and-now governance or action of God. Disciples had to be with him to learn how to do what he did.

Imagine doing that today. How would family members, employers, and co-workers react to such abandonment? Probably they would conclude that we did not much care for them, or even for ourselves.

Did not Zebedee think this as he watched his two sons desert the family business to keep company with Jesus (Mark 1:20)? Jesus stated a simple fact: it was the only possible doorway to discipleship.

Though costly, discipleship once had a very clear, straightforward meaning. The mechanics are not the same today. We cannot literally be with him in the same way as his first disciples could. But the priorities and intentions—the heart or inner attitudes—of disciples are forever the same. In the heart of a disciple there is a desire, and there is a decision or settled intent. Having come to some understanding of what it means, and thus having "counted up the costs," the disciple of Christ desires above all else to be like him.

The disciple is one who, intent upon becoming Christlike and so dwelling in his faith and practice, systematically and progressively rearranges his affairs to that end. By these decisions and actions, even today, one enrolls in Christ's training, becomes his pupil or disciple. There is no other way. We must keep this in mind should we, as disciples, decide to make disciples.

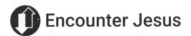 Encounter Jesus

Imagine Christ standing before you—listen as he says:

> I am the one who is love (1 John 4:8). I am the God of all comfort (2 Corinthians 1:3–4). I am the one who is humble and gentle (Matthew 11:29–30). I am the one who is moved with compassion because of the needs of my people (Luke 15:20). I am the one who encourages you through Scripture (Romans 15:4). I bear your burdens daily and support you in life's struggles (Galatians 6:2).

Now imagine that the Teacher invites you to become like him. Jesus asks you to express his love and to extend his love to a dark world. He invites you to experience his transforming love so that you might reflect his love to those around you. Pause quietly to consider this question and ask it of the Lord:

Jesus, in what ways do you want me to change? Change me, Lord, because I want to become more like you. Speak to me, Holy Spirit, because I'm listening.

Wait for the Spirit to give a specific answer and then complete the following sentence:

I sense it would be important for me to become more _____ (comforting, gentle, compassionate, encouraging, supportive, or attentive; etc.) *so that I can better love like Jesus.*

In contrast, the non-disciple—whether they are inside or outside the church—has something "more important" to do or undertake than to become more like Jesus Christ. An excuse keeps the non-disciple from becoming like Christ and the abundance of life he came to bring. Such lame excuses only reveal that something on that dreary list of security, reputation, wealth, power, sensual indulgence, or mere distraction and numbness still retains his or her ultimate allegiance.

A mind cluttered by excuses may make a mystery of discipleship or it may see it as something to be dreaded. But there is no mystery about desiring and intending to be like someone—that is a very common thing. And if we really do intend to be like Christ, this will be obvious to every thoughtful person around us, as well as to ourselves. Of course, attitudes that define the disciple cannot be realized today by leaving family and business to accompany Jesus on his travels about the countryside. But discipleship can be made concrete by actively learning how to love our enemies, bless those who curse us, walk a second mile with an oppressor—in general, living out the gracious inward transformations of faith, hope, and love. Such acts—carried out by the disciplined person with manifest grace, peace, and joy—make discipleship no less tangible and shocking today than were those desertions long ago.

 Experience Scripture

No one has ever seen God. But if we love each other,
God lives in us, and his love has been brought to full expression through us.
1 John 4:12

As a testimony of God's work in you, ask God to show you the person who needs to see his love expressed through you. Who needs you to love them, so that they can see Jesus more clearly?

Jesus, I sense you want me to express more of your love to _____, especially as I share a portion of your love in this way _____.

Talk about the changes you sense the Lord wants to make in you. Share these changes with a spouse, friend, or small group.

 W4. A Spirit-empowered disciple regularly and vulnerably shares with others how God's Word is making a difference.

Small Group: Week 1

On this day, we recommend that you spend some time sharing your responses with a spouse, friend, prayer partner, or small group. Reflect on your responses from previous days and then talk about them together:

- *I've accepted Jesus' invitation. I want to learn from him. I want to experience his love in a new and meaningful way so that I am equipped to* _____ (see response from Day 1).

- *Jesus first startled me with his love when he brought me into a relationship with himself. I am so grateful that I have a personal relationship with Jesus because* _____ (see response from Day 2).

- *Today, I am amazed at the love and grace he has shown me—especially given how he has* _____ (see response from Day 2).

- *God says that I am his beloved. That is truth. That's who he says I am. I embrace that truth most easily when* _____ (see response from Day 3).

- *I struggle to embrace that truth when* _____ (see response from Day 3).

- *I am so grateful God chose me and called me to be a part of his family. Because I am grateful, I accept his calling to proclaim Jesus and love like he loves. I especially want to love* _____ (see response from Day 5).

- *I sense that Jesus wants me to change in these ways:* _____. *I sense that he wants me to express more of his love to* _____ *especially as I share more of God's* _____ (comfort, compassion, gentleness, encouragement, support, attention, etc.—see response from Day 6).

 **Experience Scripture**

And may you have the power to understand, as all God's people should,
how wide, how long, how high, and how deep his love is.

EPHESIANS 3:18

As a final experience with your spouse, friend, or small group, spend some time in prayer. Pray over one another. Boldly declare that each of you will have the power to understand the depth of God's love and that he will empower you to live out that love for others:

God, because you are all-powerful and all-loving, I know that _____ will have the power to understand the depth of your love and will be empowered to live out that love by _____.

L8. A Spirit-empowered disciple demonstrates a consistent, bold, and believing prayer life.

Week 2

Embrace His Love

Loving like Jesus begins with our experience of his love for us. Loving like Jesus means embracing your identity as the "Beloved of Jesus!"

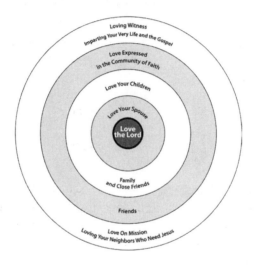

"A new command I give you: Love one another.
As I have loved you, so you must love one another."
JOHN 13:34 NIV

"A second [commandment] is equally important:
'Love your neighbor as yourself.'"
MATTHEW 22:39

Because That's Who He Is

Our ability to live out our Call 2 Love will be hindered if we cannot see the real God. What do we mean by the "real God?" At times, we all struggle to see God's true character; we sometimes have a distorted concept of who God really is. Our only hope of fulfilling our call to love him and love others effectively is to see God more clearly.

Many of us have never even considered our view of God. We have believed certain things about him and have never questioned those beliefs or been challenged with an alternative. For the next few moments, we would like for you to consider how your view of God might differ from who he really is. Here's the importance: If we are going to love God and the people he has called us to love, we need to truly **know** the real God.

From "God IS Love"

by Steve Uhlmann

The Baylor Religion Survey, published in September 2006, asked twenty-nine questions about God's character and behavior. An analysis of the answers to those questions revealed that Americans essentially hold four different views of God and his character. This was characterized as "America's Four Gods." The study noted that a person's view of God had a direct and significant impact on moral attitudes—and that this, in turn, impacts every part of our lives and relationships. It affects our behavior in ways we might not realize—though you can be sure that the people around us have noticed. Dr. Timothy Jennings, in his book, *The God-Shaped Heart*, calls this the "law of worship." We are changed by the way we view God. Jennings observes: "We actually become like the God we admire and worship" (p. 126).

According to the Baylor study, 77 percent of Americans see God as authoritarian, critical, or distant. That is, they see God as being either judgmental and angry or essentially uninterested in their lives. Not surprisingly, these groups of people either tend to become highly judgmental and critical themselves—or they have an underlying despair that God either doesn't exist or doesn't care. Apathy and narcissism are natural results of such attitudes.

Only 23 percent of Americans—barely one in four—view God as benevolent.

🧩 Engage with Your Community

"If you love Me, you will keep My commandments."
JOHN 14:15 NASB

How about you? What's your view of God? In what ways might you at times, be hindered from seeing him as he really is? Assess your own view of God and the tendencies you may have to view God in ways that may not reflect the truth about his character. Then share your reflections with a spouse, friend, or small group.

1. Do You Sometimes Have an Inspecting God?

Some of us view God as an inspecting God. It may seem as though he is constantly recording what you do on a heavenly tally sheet. Every time you sin or fail to measure up, he frowns and records it. He may also keep track of the things you have done well—but he inspects your every move and relates to you based on the number of positive and negative tally marks you have accumulated. You might imagine God shaking his finger at you, constantly using a stern tone of voice or raising an eyebrow as he examines your life.

2. Do You Sometimes Have a Disappointed God?

Some of us may view God as disappointed in us, looking down at us with arms crossed, shaking his head at our failures or lack of faith. You may wonder if you will ever measure up. You imagine that God looks down and notices you but seldom likes what he sees. That he sees your attempts at living a righteous life—but ultimately shakes his head in displeasure. You might even imagine him shrugging his shoulders as if he has given up on you—certain that you will never "make it." No amount of right behavior will ever be good enough.

3. Do You Sometimes Have a Distant God?

Some of us may see God as distant. The voice you hear when you imagine that God is talking to you may seem cold or disinterested. He speaks with half-hearted enthusiasm or great indifference. He might seem preoccupied with other things. You may believe that God is only listening to the "important people" or taking care of the "important things." A distant God seems to listen with only one ear when you pray—and therefore, you may not truly believe that your needs and concerns are of interest to him.

Look back over the three characterizations described above. Can you see yourself in any of them? On the days when you have trouble seeing God as he really is (supremely loving and excited to share life with you), which of these hindrances is sometimes true for you?

I am sometimes hindered in seeing God as excited to love me; instead, I see him as _____.

We shouldn't get too caught up in the statistics of how many people share a hindered view of God, but it does highlight for us the importance of developing a healthy and genuinely biblical view of our Creator. Fortunately, the apostle John gave us a pretty simple perspective, complete with the suggestion that if we don't experience God in this way we don't really know him:

Anyone who does not love does not know God, because God is love.

1 JOHN 4:8

Jesus made similar statements, including the most famous and well-known verse in the Bible: "For God so loved the world that he gave his only Son, that whoever believes in him should not perish but have eternal life. For God did not send his Son into the world to condemn the world, but in order that the world might be saved through him" (John 3:16–17).

There is no doubt about what kind of view God wants us to have of him. The very essence of who he is—the core of his being—is love. This is the God we ought to know—the view we need to have of God—in order to worship him in spirit and in truth.

 ## Encounter Jesus

You ... are intimately acquainted with all my ways.

PSALM 139:3 NASB

He will take great delight in you, he will quiet you with his love,
he will rejoice over you with singing.

ZEPHANIAH 3:17

Imagine the expression that was on the face of Jesus as you woke up this morning. In your mind's eye, picture Christ's kind, gentle eyes and warm, tender smile. Imagine that as you awoke, God looked down and smiled at you. With absolute joy in his heart, he announced: "I'm looking forward to spending the day with you!" The real God, who knows you intimately, could not wait to care for you today. The Creator of the universe cannot wait to show you how much he loves you! The holy God of heaven knows your darkest secrets and deepest failures—yet because of his relationship with you, he longs to show you grace (Isaiah 30:18).

What does it do to your heart to consider the real God? Tell him now:

God, when I reflect on your true character and how you cannot wait to care for me and love me, I feel _____.

God, when I imagine that you rejoice over me and look forward to spending the day with me, my heart is filled with _____.

 # Experience Scripture

I am writing to all of you … who are loved by God
and are called to be his own holy people.
ROMANS 1:7

Take the next few moments to celebrate and embrace what the truths about God's identity say about your own identity. Because he is the God who *is* love, he has created and declared you to be the one who is loved by God. **You** are loved by God and are called to be his own holy people!

Ask the Holy Spirit to confirm this truth in your heart:

Holy Spirit, would you take the truth of this passage and plant it deeply in my heart? Because I know that you are the God who is love, you have declared that I am the beloved of God. I celebrate that you have made this declaration over me because _____. I embrace the truth that I am loved by you and am called to be a part of your holy people.

Finally, what is interesting about the epistle of John is the conclusion he draws from this knowledge that God is love: "Anyone who does not love does not know God." In other words, John seems to believe that the idea of loving God is inseparable from loving our neighbor. The two greatest commandments (as presented in Matthew 22:36–40) cannot be separated from each other. This symbiotic relationship between them means that if we love God, we *will love* others. When we love others, we *do love* God. As John says, "If we don't love people we can see, how can we love God, whom we cannot see?"

> *God is love, and whoever abides in love abides in God,*
> *and God abides in him.*
> 1 JOHN 4:16

Can we really deny that love is fundamentally important—even that it is the most fundamentally important element in our lives? Jesus said, "'I came that they may have life and have it abundantly'" (John 10:10). He came to give life because God loved; because God is love. The focus of our *Called 2 Love* series is to deepen our understanding of how we are called to an abundant life, and that abundant life begins in the relational love that Jesus offers us, commands of us, and models for us.

Put very simply, if we worship a God of love, we will become loving. And if we become loving and embrace our call to love others, we will experience the abundant life Jesus desired for us.

 L4. A Spirit-empowered disciple lives joyfully and confidently in his identity as one who is loved by God and who belongs to Him.

It's an Others-Focused Love

In 1984, musical artist Tina Turner released the hit song, "What's Love Got to Do with It?" It portrayed two people trying to have a relationship based purely on physical attraction. That relationship priority simply doesn't work for the long haul. But when you truly understand what love is and pursue a relationship based on who a person is, not just what they look like, it can be the most rewarding experience of a lifetime.

A lot of people can tell you what love does and how it behaves, but they can't tell you what it is. For example, people know the Bible says that love acts patiently and is kind. They know it says love isn't "jealous or boastful or proud or rude. It does not demand its own way" (1 Corinthians 13:4–5). That's the way love operates—but what is love exactly? What is the motivating factor of love?

From *10 Ways to Say "I Love You"*

by Josh McDowell

Jesus identified the motivating factor when he said, "'Do to others whatever you would like them to do to you'" (Matthew 7:12). The apostle Paul described love this way: "In humility, value others above yourselves, not looking to your own interest but each of you to the interests of others" (Philippians 2:4 NIV). In other words, real love is other-focused.

With these and other verses, we can define what real love is. *Real love*, a love that is other-focused, *makes the security, happiness, and welfare of another person as important as your own.*

In order to love your spouse or that special person in your life, you need to know and accept why God loves and accepts you.

As a being created by God, you are worthy of love for at least three reasons:

1. God Created You Lovable

If you grew up feeling ignored, unwanted, or even despised, the people who conveyed that self-image to you were dead wrong. God makes no mistakes. You are lovable because he created you in his image—a lovable, relational image. Your lovability has been placed in your relational DNA by God himself.

2. God Created You Valuable

Anyone who says to you that you are not worth much or are unimportant is deluded. Remember, you are valuable because you were created by God in his very image. He is eternally valuable, and he has made you valuable too. You see, the value of an item is determined by what someone is willing to sacrifice or exchange for it. What was your worth to God? It was the sacrificial death of his only Son. He sent his Son in the form of a human to purchase you back. He considers you worth dying for so he can have a relationship with you.

3. God Created You Competent

Perhaps you were always the last person to complete an important task or to be chosen for a team sport. As a result, you may view yourself as incompetent or lacking great potential. But God doesn't see you that way. If you are his child, he has given you special talents and gifts. He has placed his Holy Spirit within you to empower you for service. You are far from incompetent or from lacking in giftedness. Since God has entrusted you with special gifts and empowered you with his Spirit, you can count on it: you are competent.

The more clearly you see yourself as lovable, valuable, and competent, the better equipped you are to unselfishly love. Our vision of ourselves even gets clearer when we embrace the truth of how God sees us. Let's experience how He sees us.

 **Experience Scripture**

"I no longer call you slaves, because a master doesn't confide in his slaves.
Now you are my friends, since I have told you everything the Father told me."
JOHN 15:15

Jesus desires a deep friendship with you. He desires to share with you what he has learned from the Father. You have chosen to follow him—and he has chosen to share with you, reveal himself to you, and then communicate the gospel through you.

Pause for a moment to consider this incredible privilege: The God of the universe wants to reveal himself and be vulnerable with you! How do you feel as you embrace the truth that Christ wants you to know the things that are on his heart? Respond to the Lord:

Jesus, when I consider the privilege that I get to share a special friendship with you, my heart feels _____.

Jesus, when I imagine that you want to share your heart with me, I am moved with gratitude because _____.

Jesus, because I am so grateful that you want this kind of friendship with me, I am motivated to _____. (For example: I am motivated to spend more time reading the Bible; listen as well as talk to God in prayer; regularly ask you to love others through me; etc.)

God's others-focused formula still applies, even in our romantic relationships. Here's how: When your spouse truly makes your security, happiness, and welfare as important as his own, it touches you deeply. The mark of a fantastic lover is the underlying motivation—to give to you, to please you, and to satisfy your every need because you are you.

Remember, your pursuit of intimacy goes both ways. You must choose to know the person you love and really know him or her. Discover the dreams, hopes, fears, and joys of his or her life. Understand his or her relational needs and move in to meet those needs. You will also have to choose to allow your lover to know you. Open up, be vulnerable, and share who you are—your hopes, dreams, joys, and fears. Be transparent about your relational needs, and allow the person you love to move into your life and meet those needs. And finally, choose to enter the world of your lover and be caringly involved in his or her interests. Make those interests your own as you journey through life together. This is the proven way to relational intimacy. This is truly the secret to loving.

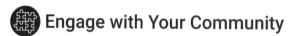 Engage with Your Community

"Freely you have received; freely give."
MATTHEW 10:8 NIV

Called 2 Love relationships begin when we stop focusing on *What am I getting out of this relationship?* and rather focus on *How am I giving?*

Loving others with sacrifice, initiative, and others-focus is a critical part of love.

Make plans to share your own story of others-focused love. Think about how Jesus has restored and revitalized your relationships—how his others'-focus has produced a measure of righteousness in you. Then similarly, tell how a decreased focus on yourself has produced positive things in your relationships. Your story might begin with these words:

I used to think only about myself and my needs in relationships. Jesus changed a lot of that. Because of him, I've learned that ...

🔆 Encounter Jesus

But God demonstrates his own love for us in this: While we were still sinners, Christ died for us.
ROMANS 5:8 NIV

God declared our infinite, unconditional worth at Calvary. Pause for a few moments and allow God's Spirit to overwhelm you with the wonder of his love—unmerited, unstoppable, unlimited grace. Imagine that Jesus is sitting beside you. Listen to the words that are just for you: *Precious child of mine, I have great news: My love has no conditions or limits. There's nothing you can do to earn my love. There's nothing you can do to lose my love. There's no expiration date; no hoops to jump through; no requirements to fulfill. I love you, period. The good news is that this love is my gift. All you have to do is accept it.*

Finish this moment of prayer by voicing your thankfulness to the Savior:

Jesus, when I read about your love, my heart feels so grateful because...

Heavenly Father, I want to be a better "giver" to my spouse/family/ loved one. Help me lift my focus beyond myself to notice the needs of others. Prompt my mind and empower my initiative to meet these needs. Empower my love for others, just like you have loved me.

 M10. A Spirit-empowered disciple lives in close, reciprocal relationships with other Jesus-followers for encouragement, support, and healthy accountability.

Because I Call You Friends

It seems strange, but friendship with God is foundational to our being a good friend to others. The startling possibility that you and I (the created) can relate closely, even intimately, with the Creator is hard to grasp—but it's true. The Bible says that Moses spoke with God as with a friend, and Abraham is referred to as a "friend of God" (Exodus 33:11; James 2:23). In the New Testament, we read how Jesus referred to the disciples and how he sees us: "I call you my most intimate friends" (John 15:15).

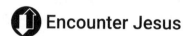 **Encounter Jesus**

Having [greatly] loved His own who were in the world, He loved them
[and continuously loves them with His perfect love] to the end (eternally).
JOHN 13:1 AMP

Despite what he knew about the disciples, Jesus declared his hope for relationship. John 13 tells us that the final evening before the passion would begin, Jesus bared his soul to those whom he knew would betray, doubt, and run away in fear (John 13:1). The one who knew no sin also knew the heart of every man and yet invited friendship anyway. As a gesture of grace, the Savior even released Judas to "go and do what you will do quickly." Jesus lovingly shared truth to Peter: "You will deny me three times." Jesus washed the feet of every disciple—the disciples who would eventually run away to protect themselves. And yet, in the midst of all he knew, Christ called the disciples his most intimate friends.

That gives hope for us. Despite what the Savior knows about us, he declares his hope for relationship. Jesus invites us into closeness with him—even though he knows there will be times when we betray, doubt or cower in fear. There will be times when Christ needs to lovingly share truth with us—but he stands poised to love us continuously with his perfect, unwavering love. Amid all he knows, Christ calls *us* his most intimate friends.

Tell Jesus about your gratitude for this kind of love:

Jesus, I am grateful that you love me with a love that's continuous and perfect—and that despite all my failures, you still call me your intimate friend. I am thankful to you because _____.

From *Love Like That*

by Les Parrott

Every social scientist knows the value of a good friend. Study after study reveals that [having] a good friend who wants the best for us—someone we respect and trust—empowers us to be better. Toni Antonucci, a professor of psychology at the University of Michigan, developed a structure of friendship represented by three concentric circles that she describes as very close, close, and not-so-close but still meaningful personal ties. The rings can play different roles, with strong and emotional ties serving some functions and less intimate friends filling other needs.

But it's the center circle where we find our most significant relationships, our closest friends who fill an invaluable role as confidant, someone who listens and pays attention, someone who is willing to help when others aren't. Someone who is invested in us being the best we can be.

These are the connections that shape our character and help us cultivate compassion. Aristotle had a name for these inner-circle relationships: "friendships based on character." He said they were instrumental in our moral development. Our close friends, according to Aristotle, shape our character. They come alongside us, for example, and help us realize that The Spirit-filled life is a supernatural life, for sure. But it requires us to do our part too. We don't just "let go and let God." We still need to step out in faith. We must take a risk. We have to open up, reach out, repent, worship, fellowship, obey, and do all the other things a life of genuine faith entails. The generous action we just made is in fact generous and not wasteful. They help us leverage our strengths and improve upon our weaknesses. As iron sharpens iron, they help us become our best selves.

And that's what Jesus is saying about our ultimate Friend, the Holy Spirit. At the very heart of our friendship circle is the Comforter and Counselor who is advocating for us to be better than the person we are tempted to settle for.

But keep in mind that as we do these things, we don't do them alone. We don't even do them by our own willpower. We partner with the Spirit. Our Friend falls in step with us, and we fall in step with him. We work together.

How the Holy Spirit Works

Someone said that many of us think that the Holy Spirit is like our pituitary gland. We know it's there, we're glad we've got it, and we don't want to lose it, but we're not exactly sure what it does. Well, the Holy Spirit does a lot. For our purposes, the Holy Spirit is our teacher, guide, reminder, comforter, and enabler. The Spirit is not a mysterious force; the Spirit is the presence of God loving in us. The Spirit is our Friend.

Some have summarized the partnership of the Father, Son, and Holy Spirit this way: The Father plans, the Son accomplishes, and the Spirit applies. Theologians may debate the simplicity of this idea, but the point I'm making with it is that the Spirit leaves fingerprints on our loving actions. The Spirit attunes us to love in ways we might never consider on our own. The Spirit is what enabled Jesus to see Zacchaeus in ways that others didn't. The Spirit helped Jesus become approachable to outcasts like Mary Magdalene. The Spirit empowered Jesus to offer grace to a woman caught red-handed in the act of adultery. The Spirit emboldened Jesus to expose the motives of false teachers and legalistic leaders of his day. And it was the Spirit who comforted Jesus in his final days to flip the script and show his disciples how to serve rather than be served as they shared a final meal together. In short, it was the Spirit who helped Jesus love others at every step.

 Experience Scripture

Dear friends, let us continue to love one another, for love comes from God.
Anyone who loves is a child of God and knows God.
1 JOHN 4:7

Reflect for a moment on how you can continue to love others whom God has placed in your life. Ask the Holy Spirit to help you tune into ways you might love that you would never consider on your own. Since love comes from God, he will be your Guide and your Source:

Holy Spirit, I ask you to show me ways to love the people in my life that I would never consider on my own. Show me people who need acceptance like Zacchaeus, a warm welcome like Mary Magdalene, forgiveness like the woman caught in adultery, comfort like Jesus in the Upper Room, and sacrificial love like the disciples. Show me who to love, Holy Spirit; I want to be in step with you.

True friendship, which is learned in our relationship with the Lord, brings blessings:

- **Friends deeply know one another.** He knows you, and you make a priority of knowing him (Jeremiah 1:5; Philippians 3:8).

- **Friends initiate care for one another.** He meets your needs, speaks with you, and stays committed to you (Psalm 37:25; 85:8; 139:3; Philippians 4:19). You listen to what he says, try not to grieve him, and celebrate his goodness toward you (1 Samuel 3:9; Psalm 100:2; Ephesians 4:30).

- **Friends vulnerably trust one another.** In Scripture, Christ shares his joys, hurts, and hopes (John 15:11, 18; 17:5). You share with him your joys, hurts, and hopes (Jeremiah 33:3; Romans 8:26).

On and on, the Master served his friends. He shared everything with those he chose to love. He chose to love you as well. Will you choose to receive everything from him? Pray like this:

Lord, you have chosen to love me completely! I am so grateful for your great love—and now, I receive it gratefully. Jesus, I want the kind of relationship with you that you spoke of in Your Word. I want you, Jesus, as my closest friend.

Engage with Your Community

Love one another, just as he commanded us.

1 John 3:23

Plan to talk with a spouse, prayer partner, or small group. Share what you sense the Holy Spirit is speaking to you about:

Because the Lord has loved me and because he is _____ (accepting of me, faithful to me, forgiving of me, good to me, patient with me, encouraging of me, faithful to provide for me, etc.), I want to worship him by telling you how he _____.

I now sense that he wants me to love _____ (name a specific person) in the same way. I plan to show some of Christ's love by _____.

L7. A Spirit-empowered disciple enjoys a lifestyle of worshipping the Lord—doing so by means of both private and public expressions of worship.

From the Father and the Son

In Christ's final prayer with his disciples (John 17:1–26), he refers to the wondrous mystery of the love that exists within the Trinity. Scripture tells us that "God is love" (1 John 4:8) and that he is "abounding in love" (Psalm 103:8). But how is this love manifested within the Trinity, particularly between the Father and the Son? The answer to this question holds significant insight into the divine plan for our spiritual formation.

From *Relational Discipleship*

by David Ferguson

Christ's final prayer in the upper room was not only for those who were present, it was for all those who would later come to believe in him as Savior, including you and me (John 17:20). In the prayer's final verse, Jesus reveals his heart's desire for us: "'I have made you known to them and will continue to make you known in order that the love you have for me may be in them and that I myself may be in them'" (v. 26). Thus, Christ prays that you might have in you both the Father's love for the Son ("'that the love you have for me may be in them'") and Christ himself ("'that I myself may be in them'"), including his love (as the Son) for the Father.

One of the most amazing blessings we have been given is this: We have received both the Father's love and the Son's love, which serve as the standard for all other love relationships.

The very same love that Jesus and the Father experienced within the Trinity is now in us. But how can we truly experience this "Intra-Trinitarian" love? And what are the implications of our experience of it for our spiritual formation? To answer these questions, let us take a closer look at the unique ways in which the Father loves the Son and the Son loves the Father.

The Father Loves the Son by Revealing

Nowhere in Scripture does the Son reveal anything to the Father. But frequently, the Father demonstrates his love for the Son by revealing things to him: "'For the Father loves the Son and shows him all he does'" (John 5:20).

The Father demonstrated love for the Son by revealing to him both the shame of the crucifixion and the joyful results of it: "who for the joy set before him endured the cross, scorning its shame" (Hebrews 12:2). Picture the garden scene, as Christ, in anguish, prays fervently, and his sweat falls like drops of blood to the ground (Luke 22:44). He looks into the cup of the sin of all mankind, past, present, and future. He entrusts himself to his Father, yet asks, "'Father, if you are willing, take this cup from me'" (v. 42). But the Father does not take the cup. The Son is to drink it all. The one who has never known sin, who was "tempted in every way, just as we are—yet was without sin" (Hebrews 4:15), is to become sin for us. Yet is it not possible that, at the same time, the Father was revealing the ultimate joy of redemption and resurrection?

Pause to consider that the Holy Spirit, in response to Christ's upper room prayer, has placed within you this same self-disclosing love of the Father. You have within you one who is longing to reveal to you all things!

 ## Encounter Jesus

He is intimate with the upright.
PROVERBS 3:32 NASB

Throughout Scripture, we see that it is God's nature to reveal. The "upright" are those who yield to what he reveals. Read the following Scripture passages below, and allow your heart to be stirred with gratefulness for the truth that God longs for you to know him.

- God has revealed himself through creation
  (see Romans 1:20 and Psalm 19:1–6).

- God has revealed both his character and his deeds through his Word, his Son, and his people (see Psalm 103:7).

- God has revealed himself through his Word
  (see 2 Timothy 3:16–17).

- God has revealed his absolute dominion over all things (Isaiah 40:21–26).

- God has revealed his desire that all his people be saved
  (1 Timothy 2:3–4).

- God has revealed his unconditional acceptance of us
  (Romans 5:8).

- God will reveal his wisdom to us if we ask for it
  (James 1:5).

- God the Father is revealed in the person of Jesus
  (John 14:9).

- God has revealed the ultimate destiny for those who follow him (Revelation 21–22).

After you reflect on what God reveals to you, pray a special prayer of thanksgiving to God, praising him for stirring up a fresh reminder of how he reveals himself:

God, thank you for letting me know you. I want to know you more deeply and to increase my closeness with you daily. I'm especially grateful that you let me know more about your _____.

The Son Loves the Father by Yielding

Nowhere in Scripture do we see the Father yielding to the Son. Indeed, the Father is always the one who commands, sends, and commissions the Son. And the Son, as a demonstration of his love, always yields to the Father. Consider the following statements of Jesus from the Gospel of John:

- "'I love the Father and … I do exactly what my Father has commanded me'" (14:31).

- "'If you obey my commands, you will remain in my love, just as I have obeyed my Father's commands and remain in his love'" (15:10).

- "'I can do nothing on My own initiative …. I do not seek My own will, but the will of Him who sent Me'" (5:30 NASB).

- "'The Son can do nothing by himself; he can do only what he sees his Father doing, because whatever the Father does the Son also does'" (5:19).

- "'I … speak just what the Father has taught me'" (8:28).

Jesus' commitment to yield was so strong that he described it as his very nourishment: "'My food … is to do the will of him who sent me and to finish his work'" (4:34).

In response to the Father's revealing, the Son yields. His yielding is so complete that Jesus says, "'Anyone who has seen me has seen the Father'" (14:9). He perfectly represents his Father's will, ways, and heart.

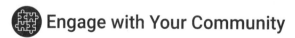 Engage with Your Community

Dress yourselves in humility as you relate to one another.

1 PETER 5:5

Plan a conversation where you talk to a spouse, friend, or small group about the privilege of receiving the gift of what God reveals and the responsibility that comes with yielding to him. Use the Scriptures above as your self-assessment. How well are you doing at yielding to the Father? Assess yourself then talk with another person about your insights:

- How are you doing at yielding to God's commands?

- How are you doing at yielding to the Father's will and plans for your life?

- How are you doing at yielding to the Father's guidance and direction?

- How are you doing at yielding to the Father as you speak, act, and live with others around you?

I sense that I might need to demonstrate my love for the Lord by yielding to him in _____.

Both the Father's Revealing Love and the Son's Yielding Love Are Dwelling in You

Again, in accordance with the desire that Christ expressed in John 17:26, you have received—in the person and presence of the Holy Spirit—both the Father's love and the Son's love. This love that dwells within us is fundamentally an "others-focused" love. We have been recipients of God's "others-focused" love: "For God so loved the world that he gave …" (John 3:16).

Having now been given the responsibility and privilege of giving this "others-focused" love, we must express it in practical ways to those near us—our spouse, children, family members, friends, and those we encounter in the course of our daily lives. We have the wondrous opportunity to express love to others in the same way that Jesus did—by receiving the Father's revelation and yielding to it.

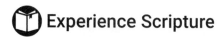 Experience Scripture

Let all that I am praise the LORD;
may I never forget the good things he does for me.
PSALM 103:2

Voice a special prayer of thanksgiving to God, praising him for a fresh appreciation for the many aspects of his revelation. Praise the Lord for the wondrous truth that his nature is to disclose himself to you. Finally, ask him to "take you into his confidence" and to reveal how the people in your life most need to be loved:

Dear God, thank you for revealing _____.

Father, I want to love the people whom you have placed in my life. Please reveal how I can love them best.

 L1. A Spirit-empowered disciple consistently practices thanksgiving and gratitude for all things and in all circumstances.

Receive and Yield

Genuine spiritual transformation begins as we recognize and embrace our purpose as those in whom the glory of God dwells, and then express his presence through our calling to love as we have been loved. We have the privilege of manifesting God's glory in the same manner that Jesus did—by receiving the Father's revelation and yielding to it.

From *Relational Discipleship*

by David Ferguson

Within us as believers are both the Father's revealing love and the Son's yielding love. The Son yielded to the Father as he was "sent out" on our behalf. Christ was empowered by the Spirit to perfectly yield to his Father's revealing love. We also have been sent out: "'As the Father has sent me, I am sending you'" (John 20:21). And because the Holy Spirit abides in us, he empowers both our ability to hear God and what he reveals as well as our ability to yield to him.

Spiritual Transformation Requires Receiving What God Reveals

Those who accept my commandments and obey them are the ones who love me. And because they love me, my Father will love them. And I will love them and reveal myself to each of them.
JOHN 14:21

The Father demonstrates his love by revealing Himself to us. The Father reveals himself through sharing his Son, speaking through his Word, and ministering through his people. In order to be transformed into his image "from glory to glory" (2 Corinthians 3:18 KJV), we need to take full advantage of these three sources of God's revealing light. The true disciple longs to receive from God through:

- **The light of his Son**: "'I am the light of the world'" (John 8:12).

- **The light of his Word**: "Your word is a lamp to my feet and a light for my path" (Psalm 119:105 NASB).

- **The light of his people**: "'You are the light of the world'" (Matthew 5:14).

As God's children abundantly receive from his Son, his Word, and his people, they are enabled to more clearly hear him.

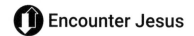 Encounter Jesus

"Be still and know that I am God!"
PSALM 46:10

Do what this passage of Scripture says and be still before the Lord. First, tell him that you want to know him:

God, I ask that you quiet my mind and spirit. Help me to focus on you. I want to be still so that I can soak in your love.

When your heart is quiet, listen to what the Lord wants to reveal to you today. Imagine Jesus is sitting next to you. He's speaking these words just for you: "I long to have quiet moments of conversation with you. I love it when you are still and free of distractions, because those are the times when you can truly feel my love. Remember, I am a God of love. So, it's in these quiet moments of time with me that I can be your Refuge, Provider, Helper, Guide, Healer, and Savior. It pleases me for you to trust Me."

Now respond to Jesus in prayer: *Jesus, I praise you for _____. I'm grateful you are a God of love who wants to reveal yourself to me.*

In what new ways do you want me to experience your love today?

Spiritual Transformation Requires Yielding to What God Reveals

"Those who accept my commandments and obey them are the ones who love me. And because they love me, my Father will love them. And I will love them and reveal myself to each of them."
JOHN 14:21

Through the gracious work of the Holy Spirit, the hearts of those who have experienced God's transforming love are inclined to yield, yearning to please the one who has revealed himself to us, longing to express and extend God's glory and express his love. The follower of Christ longs to testify, as Christ did in his final hours, "'I have brought you glory on earth by completing the work you gave me to do'" (John 17:4).

Spiritual Transformation Requires Yielding Before Receiving

We have been brought into the same love relationship as that of Jesus and the Father. Fully devoted followers of Christ are not transformed by knowledge acquired, activities engaged in, or events attended. Spiritual transformation—the process of being shaped into the likeness of Jesus—is brought about by hearing what God reveals and yielding to it. But is there anything else we can observe about Jesus' commitment to yield to his Father's will?

Recall Jesus' anguished prayer at Gethsemane. That night he prayed, "My Father, if it is possible, may this cup be taken from me" (Matthew 26:39). But consider his next words: "Yet not as I will, but as you will." Herein lies the secret to spiritual transformation: Jesus was committed to yield even before he really understood what he was yielding to. And once the Father's will was made clear, Jesus was determined to obey, as illustrated by his words to Peter: "Shall I not drink the cup the Father has given me" (John 18:11)?

In our own self-focus, we often want to know first, so we can make an informed decision about whether we want to yield. But true disciples who are eager to experience the transforming love of God will embrace a different approach:

- First, we commit to yield by faith, relying on the Holy Spirit.

- We then listen, seeking to hear God's voice and discern his will through our intimate walk with his Son, his Word and his people.

- As we come to know clearly what God reveals, we uphold our commitment to yield by following God's direction.

- Finally, we are sent out to reveal what we have received, in order that others may in turn yield to the Father.

The young Samuel should serve as our example—we are to be listening servants, committed to yield and longing to hear (1 Samuel 3:8–9).

 Experience Scripture

"Anyone who wants to do the will of God will know
whether my teaching is from God or is merely my own."
JOHN 7:17

Our commitment in faith to yield to God before we fully know is the secret to spiritual transformation. Like Jesus, we must say, "Not as I will, but as you will" (Matthew 26:39).

Are you committed to yield in this way?

We invite you to pray a prayer of yielding—to yield to whatever God asks of you, even when you do not really understand what he is asking or what he is doing.

Consider the circumstances of your life right now. Think about your important relationships.

Reflect upon critical situations and unanswered questions. What are you struggling with right now?

Compose your own prayer of commitment to yield, and then offer it to God. Use the sentences below as you pray:

Father, before I even hear your voice concerning my calling to love _____ (my husband, my wife, my child, my friend, my neighbor, etc.), I yield to you all that I am and all that my future holds. By faith, I commit to live out what you reveal. Speak to me, Lord. I want to listen.

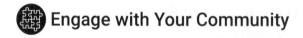 **Engage with Your Community**

Come near to God and he will come near to you.

JAMES 4:8 NIV

After you have offered your prayer and spent some time listening for the Lord, share your prayer with a spouse, friend, prayer partner, or small group. Pray for one another, asking God to answer your prayers and to come near to you and empower each of you to live out your commitment to yield to the Father.

 L2. A Spirit-empowered disciple regularly talks to and listens to God in prayer for daily decisions and direction for life.

It's a New Kind of Awesome

From *How Joyful People Think*

by Jamie Rasmussen

We want excellent clothes, excellent food, excellent education, excellent cars, excellent sports teams, excellent customer service, excellent government (no comment), excellent internet service, excellent health care, and an excellent retirement package. In our modern age, in which a level of excellence is within reach on so many levels, most of us expect excellence in our lives.

In fact, when we have a less-than-excellent experience, we make it known. A 2015 *Consumer Report* study done by the National Research Center found that nearly 90 percent of Americans had dealt with customer service in some way during the past year. Of those surveyed, more than half reported leaving a store without making their intended purchase due to poor customer service. A whopping 57 percent hung up the phone on a customer service representative due to a failed resolution. The results are in: We love the good life, and anything less than excellence will not do.

> *Fix your thoughts on what is true, and honorable,*
> *and right, and pure, and lovely, and admirable.*
> *Think about things that are excellent and worthy of praise.*
> PHILIPPIANS 4:8

The Bible's view of excellence involves two key components:

- Any pursuit of excellence must be biblically guided in both choice and direction.

- Any application of excellence must be Spirit-empowered in both motivation and action.

In other words, as people who want to be intentional in the way we think, we much approach excellence by allowing the Bible to guide us in what to be excellent in and allowing the Holy Spirit to empower our excellence as we live a God-dependent life. Only as we fuel our pursuits of excellence with these dual components can we sufficiently live out the call of Philippians 4:8 to "think excellence." Only with these two driving qualifiers can we begin to understand why the call is to determine "if there is any excellence."

🄸 Encounter Jesus

Jesus said to the people who believed in him, "You are truly my disciples if you remain faithful to my teachings. And you will know the truth, and the truth will set you free" (John 8:31–32).

Jesus guides us into deepened transformation and Christlikeness. Encountering Jesus in the Word transforms us into his likeness—a life of true excellence!

- **We can count on Jesus to guide us into truth because he IS truth.** Truth is and comes from the objective, absolute person of Christ. As John wrote: "For the law was given through Moses, but grace and truth came through Jesus Christ" (John 1:17).

- **We can count on Jesus and his Word to remain truthful, consistent and relevant to our lives.** Truth cannot be relative and change from person to person because Jesus is the incarnation of the God who "with whom there is no variation or shifting shadow" (James 1:17 NASB).

- **We can count on Jesus to be the empowerment to our calling.** Jesus didn't claim to be "a truth," one that is equal to all others. His claim was exclusive. He is the only truth, the only way to God and the one who has no equal. Here's what Isaiah tells us about our God: "'I am the **Lord**, and there is no other. There is no God besides Me. I will gird you, though you have not known Me, that they may know from the rising of the sun to its setting that there is none besides Me. I am the Lord, and there is no other'" (Isaiah 45:5–6).

Pause and reflect on the gratitude you feel about a relationship with this kind of Savior. He calls us to a life of love. He calls us to a life of excellence and Christlikeness and to consider what is also true about him:

- Jesus not only calls us to live a life of excellence, he guides us in *how* to live a life of Christlikeness because he *is* truth.

- Jesus not only calls us to live a life of excellence, he remains faithful, consistent, and without variation. We can trust in him. He is dependable.

- And finally, Jesus not only calls us to live a life of excellence, he also gives us the power to live out that calling. Our Savior guides, faithfully supports, and empowers us. What an amazing God!

Pause now and tell Jesus about your gratitude:

Jesus, I am so grateful that you have called me to love (you and others)—and you guide me, empower me, and are faithfully with me in the journey. I am especially grateful for your _____.

Because you are my God, I am motivated to _____.

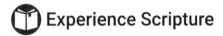 Experience Scripture

*I pray that the eyes of your heart may be enlightened
in order that you may know the hope to which he has called you.*
EPHESIANS 1:18 NIV

Claim the promise of Ephesians 1:18 that we might see and hear as Jesus does. Just as Scripture notes that Abraham was a "friend of God" (James 2:23), take a moment to celebrate that you are also a friend of God and he longs to involve you in his kingdom purposes. God is calling you to live out his call to love, and he wants to co-labor with you in the process. Celebrate that we have a God who doesn't leave us alone in our calling to love. He partners with us and then works alongside us to live out this calling. What a loving God who gives us hope!

Take time now to celebrate that you have a God who wants to co-labor with you in loving others. Ask God to open the eyes of your heart and enlighten you to the ways he wants to do that. Ask the Lord to guide you into what it looks like to live out his calling and reveal the choices and direction that fulfill his kingdom purpose the most:

God, I am amazed and filled with awe that you not only call me to love, but you love me so much that you come alongside me and help me! I'm specifically grateful for this kind of love for me because _____.

As I reflect on the privilege and wonder of co-laboring with you for excellence in relationships, would you open my eyes to all the ways you want to equip me, empower me, and express your love through me?

Continue to guide my choices and the direction of my life through your Word. Reveal to me ways that I can grow in my love for _____.

Excellence that is biblically guided and Spirit-empowered may seem like such a simple idea, but let's not rush past it. Our pursuits of excellence, guided by what the Bible says and empowered by God's indwelling Holy Spirit, are foundational to what it means to follow God in this fallen world. Pursuing excellence using these concepts is what, as the old saying goes, "separates the men from the boys and the women from the girls" in the Christian life. It is the dividing line between those who dabble in their faith and those who are all in. It's the difference between toddlers who still drink milk from a sippy cup and mature adults who eat filet mignon and russet potatoes (see Hebrews 5:12–14).

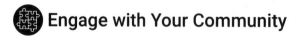 Engage with Your Community

"He who has My commandments and keeps them, it is he who loves Me."
JOHN 14:21

Our call to love (and our life of excellence) is expressed through passionate love of the Lord and as his Word is lived out with people. Reflect on a recent time when you have lived out God's Word and heeded his direction and guidance:

- Romans 15:7—*I recently expressed Christlike acceptance to _____ when _____.*

- Proverbs 15:1—*I shared a gentle response in the face of anger when _____.*

- James 5:16—*I recently apologized to _____ concerning _____.*

- Romans 12:15—*I was able to rejoice with _____ over _____.*

- Romans 12:15—*I was able to mourn with _____ over _____.*

Share your responses with a spouse, friend, or small group. Then allow the Holy Spirit to ask you often, "What Bible verses did you experience today?"

Our reputation is the combination of our behavior and others' assessments. We can't control those assessments, but we can control our behavior. Let's dream about all the various "whatever's" we can pursue throughout the day as our behavior is marked by faithfulness, kindness, righteousness, and honor. When our thoughts are focused on these building blocks, we create the right environment in which a good reputation can develop. A good reputation is something that pleases God and is certainly something he can use.

 W8. A Spirit-empowered disciple regularly experiences supernatural things as life is lived according to God's Word.

Small Group: Week 2

On this day, we recommend that you spend some time sharing your responses with a spouse, friend, prayer partner, or small group. Reflect on your responses from previous days and then talk about them together.

I am sometimes hindered in seeing God as excited to love me—instead I see him as _____ (see response from Day 8).

When I reflect on God's true character and how he cannot wait to care for me and love me, I feel _____ (see response from Day 8).

When I imagine that God rejoices over me and looks forward to spending the day with me, my heart is filled with _____ (see response from Day 8).

When I read about God's love, my heart feels so grateful because … (see response from Day 9).

Because of my gratitude for Jesus' love for me, I want to be a better "giver" to my spouse/family/friends/neighbors. I want God to lift my focus beyond myself to notice the needs of others. I'm praying that he would prompt my mind and empower my initiative to meet these needs, especially _____ (see response from Day 9).

Talk about the privilege of receiving the gift of what God reveals and the responsibility that comes with yielding to him. Assess yourself and then talk with another person about your insights (see responses from Day 11).

- How are you doing at yielding to God's commands?

- How are you doing at yielding to the Father's will and plans for your life?

- How are you doing at yielding to the Father's guidance and direction?

• How are you doing at yielding to the Father as you speak, act, and live with others around you?

I sense that I might need to demonstrate my love for the Lord by yielding to him in _____ (see response from Day 11).

Reflect on a recent time when you have lived out God's Word and heeded his direction and guidance (see responses from Day 13):

• Romans 15:7—*I recently expressed Christlike acceptance to* _____ *when* _____.

• Proverbs 15:1—*I shared a gentle response in the face of anger when* _____.

• James 5:16—*I recently apologized to* _____ *concerning* _____.

• Romans 12:15—*I was able to rejoice with* _____ *over* _____.

• Romans 12:15—*I was able to mourn with* _____ *over* _____.

Think about how Jesus has restored and revitalized your relationships—how his others-focus has produced a measure of righteousness in you. Then tell how a decreased focus on yourself has produced positive things in your relationships:

I used to think only about myself and my needs in relationships. Jesus changed a lot of that. Because of him, I've learned that . . . (see response from Day 9)

 **Experience Scripture**

So each generation should set its hope anew on God,
not forgetting his glorious miracles and obeying his commands.
PSALM 78:7

After you have shared the responses above, spend some time in prayer for one another. Declare your hope in God because of the glorious miracles and life change that has been shared. Your prayers might begin with:

God, we are declaring our hope in you because we've heard how you have changed lives, especially as _____. Because of your glorious miracles and how your people have obeyed your commands, we're expecting you to continue _____. We can't wait to see how you _____. Do it again, Lord!

 P7. A Spirit-empowered disciple expects and sees evidence of God doing miracles in their personal life and in the lives of others.

Week 3

Love the Lord

As we experience and embrace Jesus' love for us, the next step is to express our love for him. The center circle of a Spirit-empowered faith and a love like Jesus flows from daily time in the presence of the Lord with a grateful and listening heart.

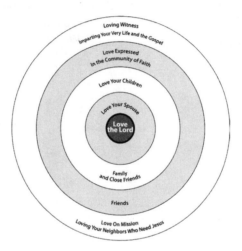

"Teacher, which is the most important commandment in the law of Moses?" Jesus replied, "'You must love the Lord your God with all your heart, all your soul, and all your mind.'"

MATTHEW 22:36–37

Can You Feel FOR Him?

Every part of our spiritual journey is either hindered or empowered by our view of God. After all, it's difficult to sustain a loving relationship with a God who we perceive is inspecting, disappointed, or distant from us. In contrast, we find that it is easy to love the God who is excited to love us—but it is difficult for any view of God that differs from that to inspire love. Our ability and power to live out our call to love will be possible only as we relate to the real God.

From *Relational Foundations*

by Great Commandment Network

Let's revisit the character of the real God by visiting the story of the ten lepers (Luke 17:11–19). As we have a fresh encounter with the God who is excited to love, we'll also have an opportunity to love the Lord.

Jesus and his disciples approach a village on their way to Jerusalem and a ragged band of men begins to call out to them. They shout their request from afar. You cannot see their faces because they have grown accustomed to hiding in shame. Days or even years of rejection have made them cower behind their cloaks. On this day, however, the rumors of a teacher who can bring healing to the sick have made the men unusually bold. Out of desperation, they call out, "Jesus, Master, have pity on us!"

Scripture tells us that when Jesus saw the men, he gave an immediate response. The Savior took one look at the torn flesh and diseased bodies. He saw the rejection and condemnation they had suffered, the sadness of their hearts as they were forced to leave family members and friends. And as soon as the Savior saw these men, he was driven to action. He was moved with compassion, and guaranteed their healing with these words: "Go, show yourselves to the priests."

Scripture records that as the men walked toward the temple, they were cleansed. Can you picture the faces of the men as they approach the city? Perhaps one man looks down and watches as the flesh is restored to his arms. Another stops and stares with amazement at the face of his friend as he sees him whole and healthy for the very first time. Their steps quicken as they remember a wife at home alone, a child whom they have never seen, or a friend who is dearly missed. They hurry toward the temple, knowing that the priest's blessing is the only thing that stands in the way of restoring these relationships that they have missed so much.

 **Experience Scripture**

O LORD, I will honor and praise your name, for you are my God.
You do such wonderful things!
ISAIAH 25:1

Take this moment to stop and do what Scripture says: Give honor and praise to God for the wonderful things he has done. Just like the ten lepers, the real God has done wonderful things for you.

• Has God restored a relationship in your life?

• Have you experienced God's compassion and initiative to act on your behalf?

• How have you sensed that God notices the cares of your life?

- How has God brought healing, provision, and relief for you?

- How has God loved you in the midst of rejection, desperation, or aloneness?

- Ask the Holy Spirit to remind you of the wonderful things God has done for you—and then give Him praise:

  God, I praise you for your goodness to me and how you have done such wonderful things, especially when you _____. I give you honor because of your _____.

Now, let's reflect on the next scene of the leper's story. Jesus has moved further down the road toward Jerusalem. The ten lepers have been sent ahead to show themselves to the priest. But as Jesus and the disciples make the turn in the road toward the city, they find that one of the lepers has doubled back. He runs to Jesus and throws himself at the Savior's feet. Tears of joy stream down his face. He is out of breath, yet his words are very clear: "Thank you! Thank you! Praise you!"

The words of appreciation and praise still hang in the air, but words have now been replaced with quiet tears. The man still kneels before Jesus, just weeping. If we look carefully, we might notice that Jesus is peculiarly still. His face is saddened. His expression is grieved. Christ kneels in front of the man, grasping his shoulders. We hear pain in the Savior's voice as he asks, "Were not all ten cleansed? Where are the other nine?"

 ## Encounter Jesus

I want to know Christ and the power of his resurrection
and the fellowship of sharing in his sufferings.
PHILIPPIANS 3:10 NASB

Pause now and reflect on Christ's question for the leper. What do they seem to suggest is in the heart of Jesus?

Jesus seems to be experiencing _____.

What does it do to your heart to reflect on the pain that Christ experienced? How do you feel as you consider what Jesus is feeling?

As I consider how Jesus must have felt saddened and disappointed because of the other men who failed to give Him thanks, my heart is moved with _____.

Pause and pray a prayer of care and concern *for* Christ. Tell him how it makes you feel to know that he was hurting:

Lord Jesus, my heart is _____ as I consider _____.

As you were able to hurt with Jesus and feel a sense of sadness for Him, you were beginning to fellowship with Christ and share in his sufferings. You were living out Philippians 3:10. You were living out your calling to love; this exercise is a part of what it looks like to love the Lord! As you came to feel compassion for Jesus and as your heart was sorrowed for Him, wasn't your love deepened for Him?

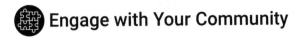 **Engage with Your Community**

Love the LORD, all you godly ones!
PSALM 31:23

Plan to share your encounter with Jesus—and to share your experience of Scripture—with a spouse, friend, family member, or small group. Declare your renewed love for the Lord:

I'm focusing on God's calling to love. I've realized that it begins with my experience of his love for me. I recently remembered how he loved me by _____.

I've also come to understand that my call to love is first to the Lord. I've recently learned that to love the Lord means to care for what he must feel. It's new for me, but my love for Jesus is deeper because _____.

 L3. A Spirit-empowered disciple develops a correct view of God as the Lord reveals himself, enjoying more and more closeness with him.

Switch on Your Brain

From *Switch on Your Brain*

by Caroline Leaf

We destroy arguments and every lofty opinion raised against the knowledge of God,
and take every thought captive to obey Christ.
2 CORINTHIANS 10:5 ESV

The ability to quiet your mind, focus your attention on the present issue, capture your thoughts, and dismiss the distractions that come your way is an excellent and powerful ability that God has placed within you. In the busy age we live in, however, we have trained ourselves out of this natural and necessary skill.

[It is *natural*] because it is wired into the design of the brain, allowing the brain to capture and discipline chaotic rouge thoughts; [it is] *necessary* because it calms our spirits, so we can tune in and listen to God. When we are mindful of catching our thoughts in this way, we change our connection with God from [being] uninvolved and independent to involved and dependent. When we objectively observe our own thinking with the view to capture rogue thoughts, we in effect direct our attention to stop the negative impact and rewire healthy new circuits into our brain.

Second Corinthians 10:3–5 is so clear in the instructions in this matter:

> For though we live in the world, we do not wage war as the world does. The weapons we fight with are not the weapons of this world. On the contrary, they have divine power to demolish strongholds. We demolish arguments and every pretension that sets itself up against the knowledge of God, and we take captive every thought to make it obedient to Christ. (NIV)

In Proverbs 4:20–22, the sage advice is to "give attention to my words; incline your ear to my sayings. Do not let them depart from your eyes; keep them in the midst of your heart; for they are life to those who find them, and health to all their flesh."

The primary success of capturing your thoughts will be to focus on God's way first, not the world's ways. And science is showing that meditating on the elements of Jesus' teachings rewires healthy new circuits in the brain.

Encounter Jesus

Fix your thoughts on what is true, and honorable, and right, and pure, and lovely, and admirable.
Think about things that are excellent and worthy of praise ... Then the God of peace will be with you.
PHILIPPIANS 4:8–9

Spend the next few moments reflecting on the parts of your life that cause anxiety, worry, stress, or heartache. Imagine those circumstances and the thoughts that go with them as fiery arrows, intent on causing harm. Talk to the Prince of Peace about these things, and then ask Jesus to replace those thoughts with his:

Jesus, I know my thoughts are not always on things that are excellent, true, honorable and admirable, especially when I think about _____.

Holy Spirit, as the guard of my mind and my heart, would you replace these unhealthy thoughts with yours? Instead of those fiery arrows, what true, lovely, right, pure, and honorable thoughts do you want me to have? Tell me, Lord—I am listening!

It Only Takes Five to Sixteen Minutes a Day

Research has shown that merely five to sixteen minutes a day of focused, meditative capturing of thoughts shifts frontal brain states. Afterward, you are more likely to engage with the world. Research also showed that those same five to sixteen minutes of intense, deep thinking activity increased the chances of a happier outlook on life.

God has blessed us with powerful and sound minds (2 Timothy 2:17). God has designed the frontal lobe of our brains precisely to do this: to handle his thought projects. This perspective is highlighted in the Message version of 2 Corinthians 10:5:

> We use our powerful God-tools for smashing warped philosophies, tearing down barriers erected against the truth of God, fitting every loose thought and emotion and impulse into the structure of life shaped by Christ. Our tools are ready at hand for clearing the ground of every obstruction and building the lives of obedience into maturity. (MSG)

 Experience Scripture

"He must become greater and greater, and I must become less and less."
JOHN 3:30

Scripture reminds us that:

- His thoughts are higher than yours (Isaiah 55:8).

- His activity is characterized by the fruit of the Spirit, and never the deeds of the flesh (Galatians 5:19–24).

- His attitude is characterized by humility and thinking more highly of others (Philippians 2:3–7).

- His priorities focus on loving the Father, loving people, and imparting the gospel so that others might embrace these priorities of his (Matthew 22:37–40; 28:19–20).

Pause and reflect on some of the ways Jesus has become greater in your life and how your thought life reveals these changes:

- *I recently had more of Jesus' thoughts when I _____.*

- *Others could see more of the fruit of his Spirit demonstrated in my life when _____.*

- *Jesus' attitude of humility and thinking of others first was evident in my life when* _____.

- *Christ's priority of love was seen in my life when* _____.

When Jesus becomes greater and when we become less and less, it will impact all of life; our thoughts and activities; my attitudes and priorities. Living out this one truth gives powerful simplicity to the focus of each day:

LET JESUS BECOME GREATER!

Our normal is wired for love. Because we are made in God's image (Genesis 1:26) and have the "mind of Christ" (1 Corinthians 2:16), science can now demonstrate that we are, in fact, wired for love.

 **Engage with Your Community**

And this is his commandment: We must believe in the name of his Son, Jesus Christ, and love one another, just as he commanded us.

1 JOHN 3:23

Since we and the people around us are wired for love, take the next few moments to plan out the ways you will demonstrate the mind of Christ and live out his priority of love.

Because Jesus notices the details of our lives, I plan to get to know the details of _____'s life. I'll do that by _____.

Because Jesus shared meals with friends and meaningful conversations with those he loved, I'm planning to invite _____ to _____.

Because Jesus accepts us when we are less than perfect, I plan to demonstrate more acceptance to _____ by _____.

Because Jesus notices and appreciates the things we do and notices the effort we make, I plan to appreciate _____ for _____.

 W6. A Spirit-empowered disciple consistently expects God to bring about life change as the powerful presence of Jesus is encountered in the Bible.

It's the Primacy of Our Faith

As we continue to learn what it means to live out our call to love like Jesus, one simple truth sums up our goal:

BECAUSE WE ARE LOVED, LET US LOVE.

Let's be clear: We are not commanded to love one another to earn or become worthy of God's love. Instead, we are called to love one another *because* we are so loved by God and have received his love. It's out of our gratitude and personal experience of his love that we are able to live out our call to love people.

Let this passage remind us of the primacy of our faith:

Beloved, let us love one another, for love is of God; and everyone who loves is born of God and knows God. He who does not love does not know God, for God is love.

1 JOHN 4:8

From *The Primacy of Our Faith*

by Darryl DelHousaye

The first phrase of the verse, "anyone who does not love does not know God," uses the verb form of *agape—agapao*. In this verse, *agapao* is in the present tense. Love in the present tense implies that we practice the characteristics of love over and over until love becomes an ongoing, continuous habit pattern.

A habit is defined as a settled regular tendency or practice. Habits are so settled and regular that we don't have to think about them. We just do them. *Agape* love is not only unconditional, it is habitual. Therefore, if we do not develop the habit of loving in this way, then John says we do not know God. Love is not something God does, love is something God *is*. The very essence of God, of who and what God is, must be defined by the quality of love. God is love.

⬆ Encounter Jesus

There's no greater demonstration of love than what Christ did at Calvary. The gospel story dramatically reveals the lengths to which God would go to draw us to himself. It was God's love for you that sent his Son to earth. It was God's love for you that sent his Son to Calvary. It was God's love for you that empowered Christ to take the sins of the world upon himself. But don't forget: God's love is personal. It's not just a love for the world. God's love is for you—individually.

God is love, and he demonstrated the depths of his love for you at Calvary. God is love—and he demonstrates his love for you on a daily basis by providing, protecting, sustaining, guiding, and comforting for you. Now ask yourself:

God went to great lengths to establish a relationship with me, and he consistently demonstrates his love for me—so how might I love him back?

The story in Bethany shows us how:

Mary sat at the Lord's feet, listening to what he taught.
LUKE 10:39

Pause and allow the Holy Spirit to bring an image of Jesus to your mind. Imagine Christ on the day when he has withdrawn from the rejection in Jerusalem and finds refuge in Bethany at the home of his friends. Picture the scene: Mary, who might have sensed the Savior's troubled heart, sits in front of Jesus. She sits listening quietly, attentive to what he says. Martha's self-focused interruption startles the quiet moment, but it also reveals a clear affirmation for Mary. Jesus confirms one way we all express our love for Him:

"There is only one thing worth being concerned about.
Mary has discovered it, and it will not be taken away from her."
LUKE 10:42

Now imagine that you have an opportunity to be with Jesus. You might want to move to your knees and sit quietly with a reverent heart. Don't speak; just listen. The Savior longs to share his heart with you. Wait before the Lord. Listen for his words of pleasure: *You have chosen well. Time with me is the one thing worth being concerned about.*

Pray a quiet prayer that is similar to 1 Samuel 3:9: *Speak to me, Lord, because your servant is listening*. Allow plenty of time to listen. You are communicating with the God who *is* love. Listening to him is one of the best ways to love him back.

When Jesus commanded us to love each other as he loves us, he wasn't talking about being nice. He specifically meant choosing continually, constantly, and habitually to recognize value in other human beings and to continually, constantly, and habitually treat them as though they have value, always seeking their good.

Too often, in real life, we find that loving others requires changing some of our old habit patterns—and we don't want to go to that much trouble. Loving my wife—that is, placing value on her—implies things like listening to her. It means proactively encouraging her to develop her innermost desires and her calling to be and to do all that God created her to be and to do. But what if fulfillment of her goals infringes on my time and my attention? I might have to change some of my attitudes and my behavior patterns for her sake.

Jesus gave his life for our benefit and he continues to stand at the right hand of the Father to intercede for our good (Romans 8:34). God is love; Jesus is God; and therefore, Jesus is love. Everything he does places value on us.

If we want to be like Christ, then we cannot separate ourselves from this question. We cannot claim to know Christ if we do not love as he loves. If we love God, we will learn to love—without conditions and as a habit pattern. If we do not learn to love—without conditions and as a habit pattern—then we do not know God.

Being Christlike is not only more important than most of us have considered, it entails changing the very core of our being until we think like Christ. If we think like him, we will act like him, as a settled and regular tendency and practice.

 Experience Scripture

You were cleansed from your sins when you obeyed the truth, so now you must show sincere love to each other as brothers and sisters. Love each other deeply with all your heart.

1 Peter 1:22

Peter reminds us that our behavior will be positively impacted because we have been cleansed from our sins, have chosen to obey the truth, and follow Jesus. We will think more like Jesus. We will act like Jesus. Peter also reminds us what it will *look like* to act like Jesus: we will show sincere love for one another.

Could this also hint at another aspect of what it looks like to love the Lord? We love the Lord when we do his Word. We read about Mary's desire to love the Lord when she said, "'May it be done to me according to your word'" (Luke 1:38 NASB). Could it be that if we want to live a life that's characterized by loving like Jesus, it will also mean that we live a life that's characterized by doing his Word?

Prayerfully reflect on the Bible verses below. Which one of these verses might you need to "do" more often? Which one of these passages, as you live it out, will be one more demonstration of your love for the Lord?

- Proverbs 15:1 – "A gentle answer deflects anger."

- Romans 15:7 – "Accept each other just as Christ has accepted you."

- Ephesians 4:32 – "Be kind to each other, tenderhearted, forgiving one another, just as God through Christ has forgiven you."

- Ephesians 4:15 – "Speak the truth in love."

- Ephesians 4:29 – Let everything you say be good and helpful, so that your words will be an encouragement to those who hear them."

- James 5:16 – "Confess your sins to each other and pray for each other."

Take time to reflect on one of these verses. Pray with your spouse, friend, or small group. Ask Jesus to make this verse true of your life and empower you to do God's Word:

Lord Jesus, I want to love you more by doing your Word. I'm asking you to make _____ (use one of the above verses) more evident in my life. I want people to see this verse lived out in me, so I can demonstrate my love for you!

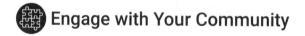 ## Engage with Your Community

Worship the LORD WITH GLADNESS. Come before him, singing with joy.
PSALM 100:2

As you have been reminded of God's love for you, let the gratitude of your heart be your guide as you live out his call to love. Ask your spouse, friend, or small group to join you in expressing love back to the Lord. Psalm 100:2 reveals one way to do that: One of the ways we love the Lord is to worship him with a glad heart.

Too often, we mistakenly believe that the way to love God is to do things for him. Instead, God is longing for us to relate to him! If God just wanted things done, he could enlist angels to accomplish his goals. We, as his created, have the privilege of intimacy, closeness, and relationship with him. Our worship and gladness provide a unique opportunity for us to love the Lord. Along with a few other people, talk about your gladness and then worship the Lord together.

I am especially grateful for how God has blessed me with _____.

I am glad God has sustained me through _____.

I praise God for his generosity and grace because he _____.

Close your time of sharing by praying together and expressing your gladness and love to the Lord. Let your prayer partners overhear your prayers of worship, praise, and joy.

 L9. A Spirit-empowered disciple yields to the Spirit's fullness as life in the Spirit brings supernatural intimacy with the Lord, manifestation of divine gifts, and witness of the fruit of the Spirit.

Through Sabbath Rest

There has never been a time like the one in which we now live. There has never been more wealth and more leisure—but there has also never been more depression, suicide, and self-destruction. Could the two be linked together in some unseen diabolical plan? Or could it be that God's plan is for His saints to come to know such divine rest in the midst of the world's harsh realities that they are able to reveal him to the world around them? Perhaps God desires for us to exhibit such a restful spirit that others come to rest in him as well. Whatever the case, we know that there is a rest for the people of God—and that we are to do our best to enter into that rest (Hebrews 4:10-11).

From *A Sabbath Rest*

by Dennis Gallaher

God, who cannot lie, promised before time began.
TITUS 1:2 CSB

So there remains a Sabbath rest for the people of God.
HEBREWS 4:9 NASB

Are you tired of the struggle? Do you look about and suppose that the God who loves you has chosen to bless others with good gifts and you only with pain?

Fear not, you're in good company. Not one person who is catalogued by faith in the Bible had an easy life. Instead, we read about lives that were marked by struggle, loss, pain, and failure, yet their stories are punctuated with this exclamation: "But God!" The litany of these faithful men and women reads like a tragic tale of loss, until God intervenes and shows himself strong, turning trials into triumphs.

God has promised you rest—and he cannot lie. Though you are bruised by the cold stones that catch your feet on what seems an endless trek, *God has promised rest and cannot lie.* Though you lie down in tears and hear only the lies of the evil one telling you that life will never change, *God has promised rest and cannot lie.* Every step you take is closer to his glory, so keep your eyes focused ahead and remember, *God has promised and cannot lie!*

Whatever path you are on is the path today ordered by the Lord, Philipps Brooks said. Faith says not, "I see that it is good for me—so God must have sent it," but, "God sent it—and so, it must be good for me."

There is a choice in rest: *Do I choose to rest in God's ultimate plan and provision or strive to get beyond the Master's release?* Choose well, friend. Choose to trust in God.

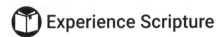 Experience Scripture

What sorrow awaits those who argue with their Creator.

ISAIAH 45:9

Consider some of the recent circumstances that God has sent your way. Are you making the choice to rest in them, or are you quarreling or arguing with God about them? The prophet Isaiah reminds us that quarreling with our Creator will only bring sorrow. But if quarreling with the Creator only brings sorrow, then how should we respond?

One of the ways we can express our love to the Father is to yield to his will and to his ways for our life. Great love is expressed when we submit ourselves to the Creator of all things—even before we know his plan for us. One of the simplest ways to love God is to say, *Yes, Lord, now what would you have me do?*

Spend some time expressing your heart to the Lord. Tell him about any tendency you have to argue and your willingness to yield to him:

Lord, I acknowledge your work in my life and I yield to it. I also acknowledge that there are times when I argue with you about _____. Keep working in me so that I would never again quarrel with you over what is best for my life. I trust that what you are doing is according to your perfect plan for me. Help me to trust you when I doubt.

The Problem with Religion

"For the Son of Man is Lord, even over the Sabbath."

MATTHEW 12:8

The Sabbath was what definitively separated the Jews from every other people group. It was not just a break in the week or a day off. It was an invitation from God to be separated totally for him. Yahweh would provide. Yahweh would strengthen and bless. Yahweh would take thought of his people as his people took thought of him. Other religions had temples, ceremonies, even circumcision, but no other religion had a Sabbath as a seal of separation to their God.

Religion falsely promises that our efforts and rules will provide for us. That is why the Pharisees were so condemning of the behavior of the disciples. And that is why Jesus' words forever altered the relationship between the Sabbath and man. No longer would men earn their "moral keep" by obeying certain rules. Having a relationship with the Lord of the Sabbath would win the day.

 **Encounter Jesus**

*"Now I am coming to you. I told them many things while I was with them in this world
so they would be filled with my joy."*
JOHN 17:13

Recall Jesus' high priestly prayer, where Christ prays not only for the eleven remaining disciples but also for you and me. One of his many requests in this prayer is that we would be filled with his joy. This is his will—that we might move away from religious thinking to a joy-filled, intimate relationship with God. We no longer have to question God's will for our lives. He has revealed it—that we may be filled with his joy.

Take some time to respond to the Lord. Share your gratitude with him about his desire for your rest and for you to share in his joy. Tell him about your desire to yield and to do so joyfully with an eagerness to please him:

Lord Jesus, I am grateful that you want rest for me because _____. I am thankful that your will is for me to be filled with your joy. I'm especially thankful for that because _____. I want your joy to be made full in me—so I yield to you, rest in you, and look forward to pleasing you.

The Never-Ending Day

*And God blessed the seventh day and declared it holy,
because it was the day when he rested from all his work of creation.*
GENESIS 2:3

It is a common thought, so old that it has earned the title of tradition. The Jewish sages noted it first in their writings about the Sabbath and many have written of it since. It is this: Each of the six days of creation ends with the finality of "it was evening and the morning." The Jewish day would begin at sunset and end when three stars were visible the following twilight. It began in darkness and ended in darkness, the day caught between bookends of night.

But the seventh day was different. The final day—God's day of rest—began but did not end as the other days. Scripture separates it from the other days by the word *sanctify*—which means "to set apart for a special purpose." The purpose of that seventh day was that God rested from all his works. All of creation was finished. All that was created was "very good." According to the sages, the day was never meant to end.

The writer of Hebrews said, "So there remains a Sabbath rest for the people of God" (Hebrews 4:9 NASB).

Spoken to the church, it was a promise that beyond salvation was a life to be attained that looked more like the garden than the world in which we live. It is the life of Sabbath, a continual trust in the provision of God that breaths out of the peace of God and inhales back his mercies. Sabbath is not a day or an event: It is a lifestyle promised, yet only obtained if we choose to enter in.

And you are invited. Sabbath awaits you today … or tonight … or this afternoon or weekend. Because God's plan was for his children to always know his rest, even during this tribulation we call life.

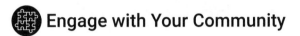 Engage with Your Community

Those who live in the shelter of the Most High
will find rest in the shadow of the Almighty.
PSALM 91:1

Talk to a friend, family member, or small group about your desire for more of God's Sabbath rest. Spend some intentional moments in quiet prayer and reflections together. Cry out to the Lord and ask him to show you the places of your life where he wants to bring more of his joy and peace. Spend time talking about practical ways to intentionally build more rest into your days, weeks, months, and years.

 L6. A Spirit-empowered disciple practices times of solitude, and prayer with fasting, in order to live out a priority of self-denial.

As You Share His Love with the Least of These

From *The God I Love*

by Joni Eareckson Tada

"The test came back, Joni," the specialist said over the phone. I gulped, waiting for the news.

"It's —negative," he sighed. My heart sank.

"Listen," he said, "it has nothing to do with your spinal-cord injury. You're just one of those type-A women who can't conceive." The words hit me like shrapnel.

Ever since Ken and I married seven years earlier, we had been trying to start a family. Now, on the verge of my fortieth birthday, in October 1989, we'd gotten the final news.

I called Ken on his lunch break at school. "I'm not pregnant, "I said numbly.

I'd always heard about the sorrow of women who were barren. Now the heartache of it hit home. I pictured the stuffed animals, the children's books, and the games I had tucked away on the top shelves of our bedroom closet. I thought of the sketch I'd drawn for turning my art studio into a little nursery, of how we would bolt a baby's car seat to a lap-board on my wheelchair. I thought of the girlfriends I had lined up to help out. And the little pair of faded-blue overalls folded in the bottom of my dresser.

People get married in order to have a family. How will Ken and I handle this?

I let large, silent tears roll down.

Sorrow hung heavy that night like a humid mist, as Ken and I lay in bed. We small-talked, but mostly, we let the silence do the speaking. Although I couldn't feel it, I knew he was holding my hand, and I was comforted by the steady rhythm of his breathing.

"So," my husband asked softly, "where do we go from here?"

For several years, I had sensed this moment creeping up. Up to now, the road had been predictable: Joni gets married, Joni has a baby—my spinal-cord injury, merely a medical bump in the road. Now it was forking off into one of those interstate highway overpasses that ends in midair, waiting for somebody to come and lay the next mile.

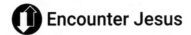 **Encounter Jesus**

"Here on earth you will have many trials and sorrows.
But take heart, because I have overcome the world."
JOHN 16:33

Pause to remember some of the times when you were faced with life's unpredictable circumstances. When have you faced some of the forks in the road that seemed to lead to uncertain destinations?

I remember a time that was uncertain when _____.

As you reflect on those uncertain times and look back to see God's provision, guidance, comfort, or the way he sustained you—ponder the promise of John 16:33. God reminds us that there *will be* trials and sorrows in this world, but our hope comes from the truth that he is with us and will ultimately overcome the troubles of this life. Our hope is not for a trouble-free life. Our hope is in Jesus!

Declare your hope in Jesus now. Because of the faithful way he brought you through life's previous trials, you can count on him to do the same in future:

God, I am grateful you sustained me through the times when _____.

Because you are faithful and because you have overcome, I am now trusting in you to _____.

Where Would It Lead?

Or maybe it wasn't a fork in the road at all. Perhaps it was a clover-leaf, curving me back around onto an interstate highway with a hundred different off ramps that lead all over the world, each mile billboarded with the faces of thousands of people I'd met over the years.

"That's all I want," I half-whispered to Ken. He turned in bed to face me. "But it's not going to happen."

"What's not going to happen?"

"A family," I said longingly. "My hopes and dreams for a family—I've got to let it go."

Ken brushed my hair with his hand.

"We've got to look at the future," I sighed.

After some time passed, I needed to check in.

"Are you still holding my hand?" I asked.

Ken raised it, so I could see.

I inhaled deeply. "If we're not going to have a family of our own," I proposed, "then why not expand our idea of 'family'?"

He turned his head on the pillow. "What are you talking about?"

"Well, couldn't it mean … your students? Caring about them. Having them up here for barbecues. Following them up as they go to college."

He thought for a moment. "Mm-hmm."

"And look at all the countries we've visited," I continued. "The symposiums in Europe we've led." The wheelchairs given. And the orphanages for disabled boys and girls. We may not be able to have our own children …"

"But we would have children around the world," he finished the thought.

"Yes—disabled children."

Ken looked up at the ceiling, thinking further.

"So," I whispered in the dark, "so why not invest our time—invest ourselves—in *them*? Oh Ken," I said as he moved closer to me, "let's invest ourselves in the children. May we please—can we not love the children of the world?"

Suddenly, the fork in the road didn't seem intimidating. That night, Ken and I decided not to live one life, but a thousand lives, offering ourselves for service in kingdom work, no matter where God sent us. The following week, I gave away most of the stuffed animals and toys in my closet, and I trashed the little sketch of my art studio-turned-nursery. We gave away the little pair of blue overalls. We decided to focus our energies on Joni and Friends and the connection we could have with even more boys and girls.

 Experience Scripture

"I tell you the truth, when you did it to one of the least of these my brothers and sisters,
you were doing it to me!"
MATTHEW 25:40

Imagine some of the moments when you have decided to live out your call to love. Remember the times when you have offered yourself to kingdom work and focused your energy on loving people well:

I remember the times when I lived out my call to love. That was when _____.

Now, imagine the divine mystery that's revealed in the Gospel of Matthew. Jesus tells us that when you were loving others, you were loving him. When you were giving to others, you were giving to Christ. When you were supporting others, you were supporting him.

Celebrate this truth and tell Jesus about your gladness—that you (perhaps unknowingly) were able to demonstrate your love for him by loving people:

Jesus, when I imagine that you felt loved when I lived out my calling to love people, I feel _____. I'm incredibly grateful that I could be a part of loving you and these others because _____.

🧩 Engage with Your Community

"God blesses those who work for peace,
for they will be called the children of God."
MATTHEW 5:9

Reflect specifically on how you might demonstrate love for others in the days ahead, specifically as an agent of peace. How could you (like Joni) help others who are struggling in their relationship with God? Reflect on that goal; plan your practical demonstration of love for others (that will ultimately become a demonstration of love for the Lord); and then enlist your spouse, friend, family member, or small group in your plans.

I plan to demonstrate my love for others, especially those who are struggling in their relationship with God. I plan to do that by _____.

M6. A Spirit-empowered disciple becomes a peace-maker who serves those who are struggling in their relationships with God and other people, working to be an agent of peace and hope.

As You Encounter Jesus in His Word

"You search the Scriptures because you think they give you eternal life. But the Scriptures point to me!"
JOHN 5:39

One of the ways we love the Lord is by encountering him in the Word and loving him as the one who wrote the Scriptures. Jesus was speaking the passage above to the Pharisees. He was reminding them that in all their religious pursuits, they had missed Jesus and the imperative of becoming "doers" of the Word. Scripture certainly provides sound doctrine and exhorts right behavior, but we must not miss out on its intended purpose: that we might encounter Jesus and see him empower us to live out his Word.

Fresh and frequent encounters with Jesus in God's Word are a powerful way to express our love to him. As the Holy Spirit brings Scripture alive to us, we are prompted to actually "do" Bible verses. It is this experiencing of Scripture that blesses the One who wrote it. Imagine the joy and love communicated to the Lord as he witnesses how he has written the Word, preserved and protected the Word … and now he finds you doing the Word!

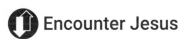 **Encounter Jesus**

Pause for a moment and imagine that Jesus is standing before you. You see his compassionate eyes and hear his gentle voice. Listen as he speaks just to you:

> I love for you to hear my Word, but don't just listen to it. Do what it says. When you live out my Word, great things happen. When you and I stay connected—I love that. My Word is a protection for you and the truth brings good to your life. I feel loved when you live out my Word. When you're not just hearer of my Word, but a doer as well, it brings a smile to my face and joy to my heart.[1]

Now respond to Jesus. First, tell the Lord that you don't want to be like the Pharisees—who missed Jesus. Secondly, tell him about your desire to be a doer of his Word:

> Lord, I don't want to be like the religious leaders who read your Word, but completely missed you. I want to know and encounter you through the power of your Word. Give me a renewed

perspective of the Bible because I know that it can lead me to a closer love relationship with you. Bring me back to the original purpose of your Word that I might daily live it as an expression of my love for you.

From *God Breathed*

by Josh McDowell

The Bible reveals an infinite God who is holy, all-powerful, and all-knowing—and yet he is intensely relational. He longs to interact with each one of us in a personal way. That is the nature of relationship; it is all about wanting to connect intimately with another—and to know that person in a real way. As hard as it may be to comprehend, our infinite, relational God has given us his Holy Spirit and the Bible, so we can learn to love and live in an intimate relationship with him.

God offers to give of himself to us, and he longs for us to give ourselves wholly to him as children give themselves to a loving father. Let's consider what Paul wrote to Timothy about the purpose of Scripture: "All Scripture is inspired by God and profitable for teaching, for reproof, for correction, for training in righteousness" (2 Timothy 3:16 NASB).

Scripture is not only profitable for teaching (right thinking) and for reproof and correction (right acting); it is also profitable for our relationships, that is, "for training in righteousness."

The word *training* is translated from the Greek word *paideia*—"to bring up," as in to rear or parent a child. This passage suggests that God's Word is designed to parent us.

Think of it this way: What is it that really parents our own children? Is it the directives, instructions, and commands we give them? Those are behavioral guidelines, but they are not what raise our kids. It is not "parenting," as a concept, that brings up children; it is the parents themselves—relational human beings—who do the work and perform that role. That is the way God designed it. He wants kids to be brought up in loving relationship.

Without relationship with another person, all attempts to instill right beliefs and right behavior will be ineffective, because they are detached from the necessary elements of personal love and care.

The Holy Spirit administers Scripture to us like a loving parent, in order to provide us with wisdom through its lessons (Proverbs 3:5), security through its boundaries (Exodus 20), caution through its warnings (Ephesians 4:17–22), and reproof through its discipline (Philippians 2:3–4). We may study God's Word for correct beliefs. We may even obey God's Word for right behavior.

But we must not forget why.

The reordering of my priorities, especially with my wife and children, has been profound due to understanding the relational purpose of God's word.

Let me take you back to what I did and what I said to Dottie one day when she was hurt by an insensitive parent of another child. It is true that my wife needed to think and act rightly. And there were plenty of verses available to guide her. But at that moment, she needed to experience God's Word within the context of a loving relationship with God and with me, her husband.

Because Dottie was hurting, I knew that she needed to experience "the God of all comfort, who comforts us in all our troubles" (2 Corinthians 1:3–4 NIV).

At that moment, Dottie didn't need to hear a passage of Scripture about how God is a just judge or how she needed to be patient and kind toward a person who had been unkind to her. What she needed was for her husband to experience with her the second half of Romans 12:15: "Mourn with those who mourn."

So instead of spouting Scripture, I simply put my arms around her and said, "Honey, I am so sorry that you had to hear those words, and I hurt for you." Dottie felt loved that day when I experienced a simple but profound truth with her from God's book. I also felt a deeper sense of love and meaning from "the God of all comfort," who smiled upon his children as they relationally experienced the truth of his Word.

God gave us the Bible because he wants an intimate loving relationship with us, wants us to enjoy intimate loving relationships with others, and wants our relationships to extend into eternity. The relational purpose of Scripture is a powerful reality—the amazing truth that God wants you to be in an intimate relationship with Him. Take a moment to allow that truth to sink in. Think of Jesus, through the Holy Spirit, speaking directly to you in very intimate terms. He longs for you to know and love him as you live out his Word.

 ## Experience Scripture

All Scripture is inspired by God and is useful to teach us what is true and to make us realize what is wrong in our lives. It corrects us when we are wrong and teaches us to do what is right.
2 TIMOTHY 3:16 NASB

When you hear the benefits of being taught by God's Word, how does that touch your heart? Allow your gratitude to help you remember and celebrate your own experiences of doing God's Word (see responses from Day 13).

Reflect again on recent times of experiencing Scripture and then describe how living out God's Word benefitted you and/or others around you.

- Romans 15:7 — *I recently expressed Christlike acceptance to _____ when_____.*
  And God's Word brought these benefits ...

- Proverbs 15:1 — *I recently shared a gentle response in the face of anger when _____. And God's Word brought these benefits ...*

- James 5:16 — *I recently apologized to _____ concerning _____. And God's Word brought these benefits ...*

- Romans 12:15a — *I was recently able to rejoice with _____ over _____. And God's Word brought these benefits ...*

- Romans 12:15b — *I was recently able to mourn with _____ over _____. And God's Word brought these benefits ...*

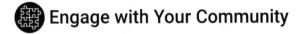 **Engage with Your Community**

Rejoice with those who rejoice.
ROMANS 12:15A NIV

Set aside some time to celebrate the blessings that come from being a doer of God's Word—not just a hearer. Get together with a spouse, friend, family member, or small group and celebrate that you did the Bible and pleased the heart of God!

- *I'm celebrating that God's Word works because I recently _____.*

- *This experience reminded me that when I do God's Word, he makes amazing things happen like _____.*

Conclude your time of celebration by praying together. Ask the Lord to equip and empower you to live out his Word even more consistently:

Lord Jesus, my heart is to bless you often through living out your Word. Holy Spirit, prompt me to ask myself this question each day: What Bible verse did I experience today?

 W7. A Spirit-empowered disciple consistently looks for new ways that God's Word can be lived out in life—looking for ways it can bring transformation in ongoing ways.

Small Group: Week 3

On this day, we recommend that you spend some time sharing your responses with a spouse, friend, prayer partner, or small group. Reflect on your responses from previous days and then talk about them together.

Give honor and praise to God for the wonderful things he has done. Just like the ten lepers, the real God has done wonderful things for you (see responses from Day 15).

- When has God restored a relationship in your life?

- When have you experienced God's compassion and initiative to act on your behalf?

- How have you sensed God notices the cares of your life?

- How has God brought healing, provision, and relief for you?

- How has God loved you as you've faced rejection, desperation, or aloneness?

I praise God for his goodness to me and how he has done such wonderful things. I give him honor because of his _____ (see response from Day 15).

As I'm focusing on God's calling to love, I've realized that it begins with my experience of his love for me. I recently remembered how he loved me by _____ (see response from Day 15).

I've also come to understand that my call to love is first to the Lord. I've recently learned that to love the Lord means to care for what he must feel. It's new for me, but my love for the Jesus is deeper because I've come to feel for Jesus as he _____ (see response from Day 15).

Since we and the people around us are wired for love, I plan to live out his priority of love (see responses from Day 16).

- *Because Jesus notices the details of our lives, I plan to get to know the details of _____'s life. I'll do that by _____ .*

- *Because Jesus shared meals with friends and meaningful conversations with those he loved, I'm planning to invite _____ to _____.*

- *Because Jesus accepts us when we are less than perfect, I plan to demonstrate more acceptance to _____ by _____.*

- *Because Jesus notices and appreciates the things we do and notices the effort we make, I plan to appreciate _____ for _____.*

*When I imagine that Jesus felt loved when I lived out my calling to love people, I feel _____.
I'm incredibly grateful that I could be a part of loving Jesus AND these others when _____*
(see response from Day 19).

*I'm celebrating that God's Word works because I recently _____. This experience reminded me
that when I do God's Word, he makes amazing things happen like _____* (see response from
Day 20).

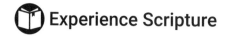 ## Experience Scripture

*Your word I have treasured in my heart,
that I might not sin against you.*
PSALM 119:11 NASB

Together with your partner, or small group, continue your love of the Lord by hiding his Word in your heart. Treasure it, memorize it, and then ask the Lord to empower you to live it. Choose one of the passages of Scripture below. Select the one or two verses you could most benefit from living out:

- Owe nothing to anyone—except for your obligation to love one another (Romans 13:8).

- But don't use your freedom to satisfy your sinful nature. Instead, use your freedom to serve one another in love (Galatians 5:13).

- Out of respect for Christ, be courteously reverent to one another (Ephesians 5:21 MSG).

- Confess your sins to each other and pray for each other so that you may be healed (James 5:16).

- Instead, be kind to each other, tenderhearted, forgiving one another, just as God through Christ has forgiven you (Ephesians 4:32).

- Give honor to marriage and remain faithful to one another in marriage (Hebrews 13:4).

- God has given each of you a gift from his great variety of spiritual gifts. Use them well to serve one another (1 Peter 4:10).

- And all of you, dress yourselves in humility as you relate to one another, for "God opposes the proud but gives grace to the humble" (1 Peter 5:5).

I sense the Lord wants me to memorize, meditate, and live out this passage of Scripture: _____.

 W5. A Spirit-empowered disciple learns to meditate upon and memorize more and more of God's Word and see it directly impacting life in a positive way.

Week 4

Love Your Neighbors

As we embrace the love of Jesus and express our love for him, the next step is to respond to our call to love the people nearest us. Loving your neighbors means loving your near ones—those closest to you.

Loving your neighbor means a priority of loving your spouse, children, family, and friends. In order to love your spouse, you have to know your spouse. Take time to know your spouse by spending time together, scheduling regular date nights or special retreats (Matthew 22:39; 1 Peter 3:7).

Your children are a gift from the Lord, who are to be valued as your most important disciples. Give time to "enter your child's world" by participating in their likes and interests.

Plan other schedules around your family's or friend's schedules. Take time off to prioritize your relationship with the closest relationships God has provided for you (Proverbs 22:6; Psalm 127:3; Galatians 5:13).

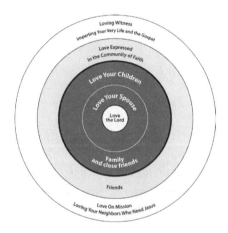

"A second [commandment] is equally important:
'Love your neighbor as yourself.'"
Matthew 22:39

Who Is My Neighbor?

From *The Art of Neighboring*

by Dave Runyon

Your life is a story—whether you realize it or not. So how would you tell it to someone else? What are the different layers in your story? And what parts are you most afraid to tell? Sharing your story, both the good and the bad parts, is key to building long-lasting relationships.

God teaches us this firsthand throughout the Bible. He doesn't offer lists of dos and don'ts to relay his message. Rather, the stories of the Bible help illustrate how he has chosen to interact with people over time. And in reading his story, we get a sense of who he is and what he is like. We begin to understand that he longs to be in relationship with us. We begin to recognize his movement in our lives as we become familiar with how God interacted in the lives of others in the Bible.

Throughout the pages of Scripture, we are touched by the story of Jesus. Christ's words were startling, and his miracles were amazing. But everything he did and said was meant to call attention to how he loved. Take a moment now to reflect on the Jesus story and how he startles people with His love:

- Jesus startled lepers with loving compassion by healing their bodies and bringing dignity to their lives (Luke 5:12–13; 17:11–19).

- Jesus startled a Samaritan woman when he broke all cultural norms and invited her to be a part of a conversation about eternal things (John 4:4–26).

- Jesus startled the woman caught in adultery when he knelt beside her, joining her at the point of her hurt and extended hope and forgiveness (John 8:10–11).

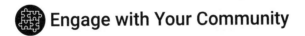 **Engage with Your Community**

I will tell of the LORD's unfailing love. I will praise the LORD
for all he has done. I will rejoice in his great goodness.
ISAIAH 63:7

Pause now and reflect on Jesus' startling love in your own life. Talk to Jesus first about your gratitude for his love:

Jesus, I give you thanks for your unfailing loving me, for all you have done, and for surprising me with your love when _____. This is a special part of my life's story because _____.

Next, share this story with a spouse, friend, or small group.

We need to recognize that every single one of our neighbors has a story as well. Deep down, we all want to share our story. We want to feel as though our story connects to something larger than ourselves. As we learn to hear others' stories, we can connect to their heart and see how God is at work in their lives.

It's about authenticity. It's honestly talking about how your walk with Jesus makes a difference. Your story should reflect not only your life before your encounter with Jesus, but also what your life has been like after your newfound relationship with him. Those around us need to hear how someone's faith in Jesus has made a world of difference. Loving others calls us to share the hope and story of Jesus.

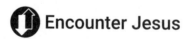 Encounter Jesus

When Jesus learned they had thrown him out, he went to find him and said to him, "Do you believe in the Son of God?"
JOHN 9:35

The ninth chapter of John's Gospel describes the best day in the blind man's life. He was healed! And yet no one—not friends, family, or the religious community—was willing to celebrate with him. The people of the neighborhood ignored him. The religious leaders accused him. His family rejected him. But when Jesus heard all of this, he went to find the man.

Take a moment right now to recall a friend or a loved one who is experiencing life alone. Jesus is calling you to simply walk alongside and encourage this person by doing life together and sharing the gospel story.

I sense God wants me to "go and find" this person: _____. He/she must feel alone right now because _____ and is struggling with _____.

Next, plan to make a phone call, send a text, or have coffee with this person and do what Jesus did. Don't preach to, advise, or give a pep talk. Just be with the person you've named above—and listen.

Ask the Holy Spirit to help you be attentive to this neighbor's story. Listen attentively to their story and then if the time is right, share your story.

We must learn to listen to our neighbors' stories. When we are neighboring well, this will happen in a natural way. We won't need to press them. Be available to enter into meaningful conversations with your neighbors, and God will open the door to further opportunity.

What does a friendly and ever-deepening conversation look like? We've noticed a pattern that often takes place over time. Conversations follow this pattern: First, we talk about the things we can see; then, basic personal information; later, our dreams and desires; and after some time, our regrets, losses, and pain.

- The things we can see include: the weather, the crazy color of the neighbor's house, the increased traffic, or the improvements to the neighborhood. We rarely enter into conversations of depth with someone we have just met.

- Basic personal information includes: How long have you lived here? Where did you grow up? What do you do for a living? Where did you guys meet? Do you have kids? Answers to these questions provide a great next step in conversation and opportunity to notice things you have in common.

- Dreams and desires: As we get to know people over time, we will share our hopes and dreams with one another. So questions like these are perfect: What do you love most about what you do? If you could do anything, what would you do?

- Our regrets, losses and pain: As we grow close to people, we have opportunities to share about some of our regrets or painful experiences. Talking about these topics first allows us to create a safe environment in which others can share their pain.

As we start to interact with people in these deeper places, we will be able to share the things that are most important to us. And if you have a deep, personal relationship with Jesus, he will be a big part of your story.

The goal is to faithfully listen to your neighbor's story, and then tell your story. After you've listened and shared your story, ask God to lead you to share his story.

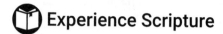 **Experience Scripture**

All day long I will proclaim your saving power,
though I am not skilled with words.
PSALM 71:15

Make it your daily practice to be keenly alert to the stories of pain and struggle of people you encounter. Listen to their story, share your story and as the Holy Spirit leads, tell about saving power of Jesus' story.

Plan a next conversation with one of your neighbors:

I would like to initiate a conversation with _____ and I plan to ask about _____.

After I've listened to his/her story and found commonalities, I'll look for opportunities to share my story about _____.

After we have progressed to a safe place in our relationship, I'll ask the Lord to lead me to share his story of saving power.

 M1. A Spirit-empowered disciple shares life with others and tells them about Jesus.

Start with a Grace-Filled Marriage

From *Grace-Filled Marriage*

by Tim Kimmel

The world we live in pushes us to live great lives. That sounds like a good idea … unless you happen to meet Jesus along the way. Then you realize that the world's advice is a trap for fools. God's Word encourages us to live truly great lives. What's the difference? A great life is about me. But as you'll see, a *truly* great life is lived for God's glory and the benefit of others.

Jesus said, "'Love the Lord your God with all your heart and with all your soul and with all your strength and with all your mind'; and, 'Love your neighbor as yourself'" (Luke 10:27). The best way to grasp what Jesus is conveying here is to see our love delivered at two levels. There's our primary love and then our secondary love. Our primary love has a singular focus; our secondary love has many objects, which we in turn prioritize in a descending order. When Jesus explains that our love for God should be with all our heart, soul, mind, and strength, he's acknowledging that it can't be all if we're sharing that love with anyone else. Plus, the words he uses—*heart, soul, mind,* and *strength*—cover the totality of our whole being when we love someone. Jesus is making it clear that he wants our love for God to be our first-in-line love—a no-one-in-a-close-second-position type of commitment.

But Jesus adds something to his statement. He adds it because, technically, they're inseparable. He says, "And 'love your neighbor as yourself.'" We could see these as two different commands—and to a certain extent they are. But more accurately, they're a couplet command. Doing the first one assumes you are doing the second.

When we love God, that love can come from two sources. It can come from our human limitations, or it can be love we first received from him and are now merely giving back. The main way we know whether the love we're giving to him is from the love he first gave to us is simple: Do we have a passionate love and concern for others—in this case, our spouse? That's what a love sourced from God looks like. We can give him all the lip service we want, but the true evidence that heavenly love is recycling through our heart is how we treat each other.

First John 4:19–21 makes this point:

> We love because he first loved us. Whoever claims to love God yet hates
> his brother or sister is a liar. For whoever does not love their brother or

sister, whom they have seen, cannot love God, whom they have not seen.
And he has given us this command: Anyone who loves God must also love
their brother and sister.

Keep in mind, here, that "brother" refers to anyone God calls us to love. I know couples who would prefer some wiggle room on this. They say they love God—even work overtime to serve him at their churches—but loathe their spouses. They assume they get a [pass] on 1 John 4:19–21 because they are so loyal to God, and their spouse is such a jerk. The Bible doesn't agree. Love that comes from God is unique: It isn't offered based on the merits of the one receiving it. Also, it's delivered in abundant quantities (more than a person needs) and graciously (as though it's an honor on the part of the giver).

Jesus set the standard for what love for a spouse should look like. His example demonstrates that true love subordinates its own position and needs for the sake of meeting the needs of our spouse. So how are you doing in that regard? You reply, "Not as well as I'd like," or worse, "Not even in the area code." Listen: You might be carrying a D-average on loving your spouse above yourself, but God's grace wants to help you ace the final.

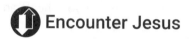 Encounter Jesus

"Come to me, all of you who are weary and carry heavy burdens, and I will give you rest. Take my yoke upon you. Let me teach you, because I am humble and gentle at heart, and you will find rest for your souls."

MATTHEW 11:28–29

Imagine that Jesus is standing before you, his eyes are full of compassion and his heart is full of love. If you listen closely, you can hear him say the words above. If you could see the Savior, you would notice that Jesus is standing in a two-harness yoke. One side of the yoke is around Jesus, while the other is empty. Christ extends his invitation to you: *Take my yoke upon you, my beloved. This simple tool was used long ago, but its symbolism applies today. A yoke was used on a farm for more experienced animals to teach the young ones. So learn from me. Let me teach you how to love your spouse well.*

This is your invitation to join Jesus, to partner with the one who is love in order to give his love to others. In your own mind and heart, picture yourself rising to join Jesus in the yoke. Imagine yourself standing alongside the one who is love. Talk to Jesus about your willingness to join him in the yoke and your desire to learn from him. Thank him that he will be your teacher and your guide.

Engage with Your Community

Plan a time to share about this moment with your spouse. Tell your husband or wife about your commitment to join Jesus in loving well. Your words might begin with these:

I've spent some time with Jesus in prayer. He invited me to join him in loving well. Because I love you, I've asked the Lord to show me how to _____.

True greatness is a passionate love for Jesus Christ that shows itself in an unquenchable love and concern for others.

This is what the Bible teaches should be the overarching goal of our lives.

> Christ's love compels us, because we are convinced that one died for all, and therefore all died. And he died for all, that those who live should no longer live for themselves but for him who died for them and was raised again. So from now on we regard no one from a worldly point of view. Though we once regarded Christ in this way, we do so no longer. Therefore, if anyone is in Christ, the new creation has come: The old has gone, the new is here! All this is from God, who reconciled us to himself through Christ and gave us the ministry of reconciliation: that God was reconciling the world to himself in Christ, not counting people's sins against them. And he has committed to us the message of reconciliation. (2 Corinthians 5:14–19)

We are not driven by our love for God but by his love for us. God's love for us is the only thing that can carry us through all that life throws at us, as well as keep all our other priorities in balance—especially our marriage. Our love for him, though well intended, is still drawn from a bank account with credit limits. That's why the love we must give our spouse is the love God pours over us each second of our life.

God's love is an extension of his amazing grace. This love/grace has a compelling nature to it—meaning, among other things, we can't truly receive it and [do] not also want to send it back outwards to others. That's because God's grace transforms. It reboots. It does not leave us the same way it found us.

 ## Experience Scripture

The Bible clearly reminds us "not to receive the grace of God in vain" (2 Corinthians 6:1 ESV). God does not want us to take the gifts he has given for granted. His grace is a gift of unmerited favor. The gift of your spouse is a gift from the Lord:

- Husbands, you have been gifted with a wife (Proverbs 18:22).

- Wives, your husband is one of God's gifts from above (James 1:17).

Take a few moments to pray in the confident faith of 1John 5:14–15. Pray a prayer that you can be certain is according to God's will. Pray with sincerity:

Lord, I receive my wife/husband as a gift from you. I recommit myself to joining you in treating my partner as a treasured gift. I don't want to take this gift for granted, so I recommit to living out my call to love my spouse. Please continue to build our home and marriage according to your desires.

 P5. A Spirit-empowered disciple consistently shows family and close friends the kind of love that Jesus has for those he loves.

Learn the Language of Love

From *The Language of Love*

by Gary Smalley and John Trent

Study after study has reached the same conclusion: An essential part of an intimate marriage is found right at our fingertips. Among many others, UCLA researchers have concluded that meaningful touch is crucial to the formation and preservation of an intimate relationship. In fact, research has shown that a woman needs 8 to 10 meaningful touches each day just to maintain physical and emotional health.

Since many husbands don't understand how important touching is to a woman, it's safe to say that many wives' needs are unmet. The result is that outside the bedroom, a woman must often look to her children, relatives, or supportive friends to make up for a lack of meaningful touch from her husband.

Many husbands don't understand that by depriving a woman of nonsexual touching, they're opening the door for another man to provide that missing fulfillment. That door never needs to be left open. Men need to realize that more than 80 percent of a woman's desire for meaningful touch is nonsexual. For example, holding hands while in line, giving an unrequested back rub for a few moments, gently stroking her hair (in the right direction!), and hugging her tenderly are all ways to build intimacy in a relationship.

Consistent, gentle touching is one of the most powerful ways to increase feelings of security, prime the pump for meaningful conversation, and set the stage for emotionally bonding and romantic times. Communication studies show that nonverbal messages are more powerful than verbal ones. Because of the incredible emotional weight of meaningful touching, the nonverbal picture of a hug left in a person's mind can solidify a relationship—just as it did for a man who called us one day on a radio talk show and told his remarkable story.

We were on one of our favorite call-in programs in Southern California. With his sensitive style, the host asked us to explain a relationship principle and would then encourage listeners to call with their problems, questions, or comments. We had just finished explaining the significance of meaningful touch when a man we'll call Daniel phoned us.

"When I was 51 years old, I suffered a major heart attack," he said. "I was rushed to the hospital, and because the attack was so severe, my wife called my father to come to my bedside. To my knowledge, my dad never told me he loved me. Nor did he ever say he was proud of me. He was always there and always supportive in his quiet way, but I still left home questioning whether he really loved and cared for me."

"But as I lay in that hospital bed, with the doctors telling me that I might not make it, my 70-year-old father was flying across the country to be at my side. He arrived the day after my heart attack, and when he came into my room, he did something I will never forget. He pulled up a chair next to my bed, sat down, and then took my hand in his. I couldn't remember him ever hugging or kissing me, but as I lay there in intensive care, with tubes running everywhere, he stayed for several hours, much of that time just holding my hand."

Up to that point, we thought we were hearing just another dramatic example of the powerful, symbolic picture that meaningful touch can leave behind. We weren't expecting what he said next:

"It still hurts to a degree that my father never said he loved me. But by reaching out and holding my hand, he expressed what he could never put into words. And it was just what I needed to know, because two days after he flew out to be at my bedside, he died of a stroke."

We adjusted our headphones to make sure we'd heard him correctly.

"I was the one expected to die, but I recovered, and my father died," he said. "But when he came to my hospital room, he left me something for which I will always be thankful. When he held my hand, he shouted the words he could never speak—words of love that I saw in his eyes and felt through his hands."

In a marriage, you can also leave lasting pictures of love for your spouse. Your gentle acts of touch, no matter how small, can impart an indelible image of commitment and unconditional acceptance that supports an intimate marriage for a lifetime.

 ## Encounter Jesus

Have this attitude in yourselves which was also in Christ Jesus.

PHILIPPIANS 2:5 NASB

Allow the power of this story to impress you with this truth: Of the seven billion people on the face of this planet, no one has been called to love your spouse more than you! So how will you better express your love to your husband or wife?

Could God want to change your attitude about your relationship with your spouse? Could Jesus want to renew the way you see your partner—not as a problem to be fixed or tolerated, but as a gift to be cherished?

Ask God to show you any changes that might need to be made:

Jesus, show me any attitudes that are true of Jesus that need to be true of me, especially in relationship with my spouse. I want our marriage to be an example and blessing to our children. I want our marriage to reflect your love. Speak to me, Lord. I am listening …

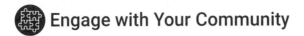 **Engage with Your Community**

Be humble, thinking of others as better than yourselves.
PHILIPPIANS 2:3

Plan to share what the Lord reveals to you with your spouse. Talk to your partner about the changes you sense the Lord wants you to make *and* ask for your spouse's input. Humble yourself and enlist your partner's feedback:

In my prayer time recently, I asked God to show me things in my life that need to change, I sensed that God wants me to change my _____ and make me more _____ (affectionate, sensitive, patient, supportive, etc.).

I would also like to hear from you. How can I love you more? Could you let me know one way I could do a better job of conveying my love for you?

Listen with openness and humility. Be ready for God to give you the power to live out this call to love!

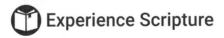 **Experience Scripture**

Let no unwholesome word proceed from your mouth, but only such a word as is good for edification according to the need of the moment, so that it will give grace to those who hear.
EPHESIANS 4:29 NASB

Living out your call to love—especially with your spouse—will require a language of love. Living out your call will require that you pause and consider the words you say about your spouse.

Take a moment to think about your spouse. What specific character qualities do you admire in him/her? What positive character traits have you noticed, and when have these traits been demonstrated? Plan how you will finish this sentence about your partner:

I admire your _____. And I see this quality in you when _____.

- For example: *I admire your enthusiasm. I see this quality in you when we work together in the yard. You are always excited to see the finished product and enjoy being outdoors.*

- Or, *I admire your patience. I see this quality in you when you talk about the difficult relationships at work.*

Here's a list of character qualities. Be ready to share one of these qualities with your spouse or voice one of your own:

- Boldness
- Compassion
- Contentment
- Creativity
- Determination
- Diligence
- Discernment
- Endurance
- Fairness
- Faith
- Flexibility

- Generosity
- Gentleness
- Gratefulness
- Initiative
- Integrity
- Loyalty
- Responsibility
- Sensitivity
- Sincerity
- Understanding
- Wisdom

 P1. A Spirit-empowered disciple lives as an example of doing good things toward all people.

Includes Loving Your Spouse

From *Loving Your Spouse When You Feel Like Walking Away*

by Gary Chapman

I met Dale at one of my marriage seminars in Iowa. He was a pig farmer and extremely successful in business. "If raising pigs and making money could ensure a good marriage," he said, "I would have one."

He went on to explain, "I consider myself a strong man. I don't usually let things get me down, but my wife's constant criticism has almost destroyed me. Other people can get on my case, and I let it roll off like water on a pig's back, but when my wife constantly criticizes me it is like a dagger in my heart.

'She's so negative, not only toward me but toward everyone and toward life in general. She stays depressed a lot of the time.... Her life is miserable, and she tries to make my life miserable. I find myself wanting to stay away from the house and not be around her. I know that's not the answer. It has affected our sex life and everything. I don't want to leave my wife. I know she needs help, but I don't know how to help her."

After hearing Dale's story, I strongly urged him to seek counseling on how he could become an agent of positive change in his marriage. He countered that the nearest counselor was fifty miles away. I assured him that it would be worth the drive.

Two years later, I was greatly encouraged when I returned to Iowa for another marriage seminar and saw Dale again. (He had driven one hundred fifty miles to attend the seminar.) This time his wife was with him, and at one of our break times he told me what had happened over the past two years.

Dale's first discovery in the counseling process was finding out why his wife's critical words had been so painful to him. Two factors gave him this insight.

The first discovery that helped him came from recalling his family of origin. Dale had absorbed a lot of critical words from his family growing up. He could never do anything to his father's satisfaction. Thus, Dale grew up with the feeling of inadequacy. As a boy, the message playing in his mind ran something like: *When I get to be a man, I will be a success. I will prove my dad wrong, and I will get recognition.*

In adulthood, Dale had lived out that dream. His hard work and commitment had paid off; he was a successful farmer and was known not only in the county but also in the state. He was indeed respected by his peers, but the person whose affirmation he most desired, namely his wife, only echoed his father's condemning messages. What he had worked all his life to overcome was staring him in the face every day.

The second insight that helped Dale understand himself was the discovery that his primary love language is words of affirmation. The thing that genuinely makes him feel loved and appreciated is hearing affirming words. Thus, his wife was speaking a hostile, foreign love language as she gave him condemnation instead of affirmation. Her words stung more deeply because he was suffering from an empty love tank. Her critical words were like bullets piercing the love tank itself. He was emotionally devastated.

Dale also discovered something about his wife's needs. Erika was operating out of her own unmet emotional needs. He learned that her primary love language was quality time, and that because of the long hours required on the farm and his strong desire to be a successful farmer, he had little time left over for her. In the earlier days of the marriage, Erika had begged him to spend time with her, to take her to a movie, to attend the church picnic with her, or to take a vacation in the summer. But he had been too busy for such things.

Now Dale realized that he had not spoken his wife's principle love language for years. And he now realized that her critical words were desperate cries for love. Erika's verbal abuse had grown out of her sense of hopelessness in the marriage, and her growing lack of interest in their sexual relationship was stark evidence that she felt little emotional love coming from him.

"I finally got it," Dale said. "So I was able to help Erika. I shared with her that I was learning a lot about myself and about marriage from my counselor. I told her that I recognized that in many ways I had not been a good husband and that with God's help I wanted to change that."

"She was shocked the morning I told her that I would like for us to go on a picnic at the lake near us," he said. "We spent three hours together, walking, sitting, and talking. I told her how sorry I was that I had spent so little time with her through the years and that I wanted us to make the future different. She opened up and told me her pain from past years. But this time she wasn't being critical, just honest about her need for love. Toward the end of the afternoon, we found ourselves hugging and kissing. It almost seemed like we were dating again."

 Encounter Jesus

The righteous cry out, and the LORD hears them;
he delivers them from all their troubles.
PSALM 34:17

Reflect on your own relationships. Do you have any moments that are similar to Dale? You love this person but have no idea how to demonstrate that love in meaningful ways. When we run out of love for people, it's time to turn to the God who is love. Cry out to him, tell him about your struggle, and be confident that he hears you and will deliver you from your trouble:

Lord, I am struggling to love _____. It is hard for me to _____.

Now listen to what the Lord has to say to you. Imagine that he is sitting next to you and saying these words:

> *If you are struggling with relationships, come to me and let my unfailing love surround and comfort you. Pour out your heart to me, because I promise to hear you and deliver you. I not only care about the anguish of your soul; it makes my heart sing to give you strength. Because you are the one I love, I will refresh you when you are weary, and I will satisfy you when you are faint.[2]*

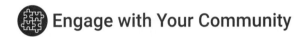 Engage with Your Community

Yes, each of us will give a personal account to God.
Romans 14:12

Reflect on Dale's story above and ask the Lord to show *you* any areas of healing that are needed in your relationship. Ask God:

God, please show me any ways I have hurt _____. I want to give a personal account of how I am caring for the loved ones you have given me. Show me the areas of my relationship that need to be healed.

Next, talk to a trusted friend, mentor or prayer partner about these insights. Get their insight about areas you need to confess or ways you need to grow and change. (This is not the time to talk about how another person needs to change). If you're married, talk with this person about your ability to live out your call to love your spouse and ways you need to change. If single, talk with this person about your ability to live out your call to love with your kids, friends, family, or co-workers.

 Experience Scripture

Confess your sins to each other and pray for each other
so that you may be healed.
JAMES 5:16

Prayerfully ask the Lord to reveal and empower your confession. Ask him to show you the ways that you have hurt your loved one and to help you do what Scripture says. Confess these things to one another and then pray for that person. Your confession might sound like:

I was wrong when _____; or, I deeply regret that I _____.

I know you must have felt _____ when _____.

Will you forgive me?

After you and your partner have shared all that needs to be shared, pray for God to heal this person's hurt: *Could I pray for you and ask God to heal this hurt for you?*

 W9. A Spirit-empowered disciple lives in freedom, not struggling with hurt from the past or fear of the future; and consistently experiences God's Word in order to bring healing to the hurt and pain in life.

Maintenance Is a Must

From *Extreme Home Makeover*

by Terri Snead

Healthy relationships need constant attention and a commitment to personal responsibility. Avoiding extreme repairs to relationships requires that each of us give a frequent account to God for our own choices and behavior (Romans 14:12). We often think that only conflicted relationships need attention, but the healthiest relationships are constantly worked on and carefully maintained. Every type of relationship will benefit from the following scriptural principles that teach us how to keep relationships healthy and whole.

Here is an important tool for loving like Jesus in your closest relationships.

> *Don't let the sun go down while you are still angry.*
> EPHESIANS 4:26

In relationships where there's a love like Jesus, individuals deal immediately with any misunderstanding, hurt, or issue that might promote anger. The passage suggests that anger should not be internalized or go unresolved because unresolved hurt may lead to the painful emotions of bitterness, fear, guilt, condemnation, and despair. We can see how God's admonition in Ephesians is meant for our good because these painful emotions have been linked to insomnia, high-blood pressure, anxiety, and headaches. There are no perfect relationships. All relationships will inevitably experience hurt or conflict, and yet it is our reluctance to deal with these conflicts promptly that can cause us to internalize negative emotions that God never intended for us to bear. Jesus has a master plan for maintaining close relationships. It's up to us to use his tools!

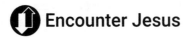 **Encounter Jesus**

> *Make allowance for each other's faults and forgive anyone who offends you.*
> *Remember, the Lord forgave you, so you must forgive others.*
> COLOSSIANS 3:13

Ask the Holy Spirit to show you any unresolved anger, bitterness, and resentment. Spend the next few moments in prayer, asking God to reveal any of these painful emotions in your life.

I sense that I may still be angry about _____.

Now, imagine the scene of Calvary—Christ on the cross. Remember Jesus' words: "'Father, forgive them, for they don't know what they are doing'" (Luke 23:34). Allow your heart to be touched with gratitude and wonder that you have received his gift of forgiveness. Despite your sin, all the ways you have fallen short, in spite of all the ways your sin has hurt Jesus, you have been forgiven. That's what the cross is all about!

Allow your heart to be touched again with gratitude and wonder that you have received Christ's gift of grace and forgiveness. You have been granted forgiveness—even though your choices, your behavior and your wrong-doing have been a part of why Christ had to die.

Voice your prayer of gratitude for how you have been forgiven, then ask God to speak to you about any ways you need to forgive others:

Jesus, I am grateful for your forgiveness of me. I'm especially humbled that You would forgive me, despite _____.

Jesus, I know that your Word tells me to make allowance for other's faults and to forgive as you have forgiven me, so I'm asking you to help me forgive _____ because _____. I choose to forgive and make allowances because you have done the same for me.

God wants us to grow up, to know the whole truth and to tell it in love.
Ephesians 4:15 MSG

Maintaining close relationships and loving like Jesus means dealing with conflict by sharing truth and sharing truth with a motive of love. This Bible verse tells us what to speak: the truth. Whenever there is a conflict in interpersonal relationships, seek the truth. Many times, a lack of accurate information leads to our relational conflict. Therefore, talking through a situation, getting the facts, and clearing the air will dissolve many conflicts. Proverbs 18:17 says, "The first to present his case seems right, till another comes forward and questions him" (NIV). This proverb reminds us: There are always two sides to every story.

Ephesians 4:15 also speaks about how the truth should be spoken and how it should be delivered. Armed with the truth, we are not to wield it as a weapon, using the truth to destroy or hurt other people. We must share the truth in love. This means that as we speak truth to another person, it must be done with a respectful tone of voice and with an agenda of restoring peace within the relationship.

If we ignore either admonition in Ephesians 4:15, we can bring destruction to a relationship. If we are reluctant to share the truth, choosing instead to "hide" it, our relationships are susceptible to anger, bitterness, guilt or fear. If we ignore the admonition to share truth in love, our relationships are prone to more conflict because of our tendency to "hurl" the truth at others. "Hiders" don't' share the truth. "Hurlers" share the truth but not in love. Both approaches can produce disastrous results. "Healers" share the truth in love.

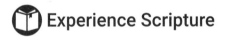 Experience Scripture

Instead, we will speak the truth in love,
growing in every way more and more like Christ.
Ephesians 4:15

Look for an opportunity this week to speak the truth in love. Think about a relationship in which you could "wish for more or something different." Share these words with a friend, spouse, co-worker, or loved one:

I would really enjoy it if we could _____. Or, It would mean a lot to me if we could _____.

- For example: *I would really enjoy it if we could have lunch together this week. I've been missing our time together.*

- Or, *It would mean a lot to me if could all help with the chores after dinner.*

Watch as God's formula for maintaining closeness in relationships comes about!

Engage with Your Community

A gentle response defuses anger,
but a sharp tongue kindles a temper-fire.
PROVERBS 15:1

In relationships where a love like Jesus is prioritized, individuals learn to diffuse volatile conversations with gentle responses. Speaking a gentle answer doesn't mean that you or your needs don't matter; it's not an opening for another's verbal abuse or inappropriate behavior. Neither does it mean that others can express their anger without restraint. Proverbs 15:1 is best applied to the first moments of a conflicted conversation. Giving a gentle answer can diffuse an explosive situation before it gets out of control. Once a conversation is manageable, reconciliation is possible.

Think about a conversation that could prevent or redirect a potential conflict. Write out a "gentle answer" that could move away from conflict and toward reconciliation. What gentle answer could you give that might diffuse a tense situation?

After you've written out your response, share it with a spouse, friend or family member. Practice your response and ask for your partner's feedback. Is your response a true, "gentle answer?"

Finally, pray together and ask God to empower your next conversation and fill it with peace because of your gentle answer.

 W2. A Spirit-empowered disciple loves God's Word and lives it out—doing what it says, not just hearing or knowing what it says.

Live Worthy of Honor

*"Honor your father and mother. Then you will live a long,
full life in the land the Lord your God is giving you."*
Exodus 20:12

This commandment is easy for some, and challenging but possible for others. Yet it stands as God's will for children of every age and all circumstances. So much is lost when we neglect this command: the emotional connection of expressed love, the bonding of generations, the healing of past pain, and the real possibility of family reconciliation.

From *The Forgotten Commandment*

by Dennis Rainey

*A good character is the best tombstone. Those who loved you and were helped by you will
remember you. So carve your name on hearts
and not on marble.*
C.H. Spurgeon

Years ago, I had an unusual speaking opportunity. First, I addressed a group of teenagers, exhorting them to heed the command of Ephesians 6:1–3, which instructs children to *obey and honor* their parents. Then I had the opportunity to speak about the same passage to the parents of those teens. But the moment I'll never forget from that gathering was when a psychiatrist posed this question to those parents: "Are you worthy of honor?"

I remember the room was strangely quiet. Most had never considered the question. And many had to answer with a sheepish, "No … I'm really not worthy."

How can you make it as easy as possible for your children to honor you?

It's been fascinating to read through the special tributes that adult children have written for their parents over the years. The memories in these tributes formed a mosaic of what a family ought to be. Over and over, the children who wrote tributes considered three things important:

- Their parent's involvement

- Their parent's emotional support

- Their parent's character

Let's consider how we can become a parent worthy of honor by building each of these qualities into our lives.

Principle #1: Your children will remember your involvement.

Your children need more than your time; they need your attention. They flourish when you focus on them. This means more than just showing up at soccer games. Children need your heart knitted to theirs as they make choices and hammer out their character. They need you to know what's going on in their lives. They need you to help them think about the clothing they wear, the type of person they date, and the peer pressure they face.

In order to be a parent worthy of honor, you can't just *be* there—you have to be **all** there.

That sounds simple—but it's easy to fill your hours away from work with television shows, the Internet, hobbies, finances, books, shopping, and housework. If you were able to add up how much time you actually spend focusing on your children each week, you might be shocked to discover that your total would be measured in minutes, not hours.

Being all there does not mean you do it perfectly every time, but it does mean that you are keeping the lines of communication firmly open and intact.

 **Encounter Jesus**

Thanks be to God for His indescribable gift.

2 CORINTHIANS 9:15

Take a moment and reflect on Jesus. His very nature is to be with and give to us. He is determined to be "all there" for us despite our selfishness and our prideful self-reliance. He gives in the face of our competition, comparisons, and division. Jesus was all there for us—even in the face of our sin (Romans 5:8).

What do you feel as you consider Jesus' response to you? How is your heart stirred by the knowledge of how he longs to be with you? How are you affected as you sense that Jesus is "all there" for you, wanting to love you and give to you?

Express your gratitude for the heart of Jesus that gives first:

Jesus, I am grateful for your heart of love, a love that gives _____. I am overwhelmed by feelings of _____. I want the love that I have received from You to empower my love for _____.

Principle #2: Your children will remember your emotional support.

I will never forget a counseling appointment many years ago. A mom sat in my office and told the story of her eleven-year-old son's relationship with his dad. The father—a hard driving and successful businessman—constantly criticized the boy:

"You dummy, you left the door open"

"Look at these grades! That's pitiful!"

"You struck out at the game! I can't believe you did that!"

By my estimate that boy is in his late forties now. And I'll bet he still hears an inner recording repeatedly playing. "You're a failure! You can't do it! Why try?"

Some of you know how painful it feels to hear that inner recording day after day. Is this the type of recording you want for your children?

Reading through tributes, I've also observed how adults do remember the positive emotional support they received from their parents:

I can't remember a time that you didn't accept me. I was always OK. My performance was OK too, as long as I tried my hardest.

You encouraged me to develop the talents God had given me. You told me about how it thrilled you to feel me stir within you before I was even born whenever music was being played at church. You were always there to encourage me in my lessons and to shine with pride at my success.

How often do you tell your children you love them, or that you forgive them? Your kids should hear these words so often that they should have no idea how often you've said them.

Another way to give your children emotional support is by utilizing the power of the printed word. Letters and notes are tangible reminders to your children that you love and care for them. Young children, especially, will treasure your handwritten notes of affection.

Emotional support is also felt when we physically touch our children. Hugs, tight embraces, and kisses are all the steady practice of a parent who wishes to be worthy of honor. I've found that if dads give physical and emotional affection when their children are young, it won't be nearly as difficult when they become teens. It's difficult sometimes to hug teenagers because they act like they don't need it. But that's just a facade.

I'll never forget Barbara hugging our son Benjamin after a rough day at his junior high. She let go; he didn't. He was admitting, nonverbally, "I may be nearly as tall as you, and I may look grown up, and I may act like I don't need affection, but I do!" By filling and refilling our child's emotional tank, you and I become worthy of honor.

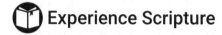 Experience Scripture

Now that you have purified yourselves by obeying the truth …
love one another deeply, from the heart.
I Peter 1:22 NIV

How might you better express Christ's love to your children? Make plans to show love to your child in one of these four ways. You might write a note or share these words in person:

Appreciation (for things they do):

_____ *(Say the name of each child), I appreciate all that you do to make our family great. I've especially noticed how you _____. Thank you for the way you help with _____.*

Encouragement (during a struggle):

_____, *I know that it's been hard to_____ but I know you can _____.*

I want to encourage you in _____ because I believe in you and know that you _____.

Celebration (of a positive event in their life):

_____, *I am so happy that you _____. It makes me smile to know that _____. I'm excited that you _____.*

Comfort (about a painful event/issue in their life)

_____, I'm so sorry that you're going through this _____. I feel a lot of compassion for you because _____.

Pause now to ask Jesus to empower you to express love to your children deeply and frequently.

Principle #3: Your children will remember your character.

As a parent, you have the incredible responsibility of shaping the moral conscience of the next generation. Even though your children will grow up to make their own choices, the character qualities you model and teach will help mold them and give them direction. In fact, I've noticed that many children, after passing through years of rebellion against their parents, settle into adulthood by adopting many of the same character qualities that they once railed against.

Once again, I found these character qualities highlighted often in the tributes I've read. For instance: "You taught me through example to honor and respect my elders, to establish a strong work ethic, and to complete a task with excellence. You are a man of your word."

What character qualities do you want to pass on to your children? What do you believe in? What are your core values?

The Roman philosopher Seneca said,

YOU MUST KNOW FOR WHICH HARBOR YOU ARE HEADED IF YOU ARE TO CATCH THE RIGHT WIND TO TAKE YOU THERE.

If you've determined what your core values are, then you can find creative ways to teach and model them to your children.

God will help you be worthy of honor and involved in your child's life. Just ask him to reconnect your heart to your children's.

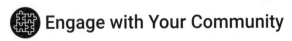 **Engage with Your Community**

This is the confidence we have in approaching God: that if we ask anything according to His will, He hears us. And if we know that He hears us—whatever we ask—we know that we have what we asked of Him.

I JOHN 5:14

After you have effectively prioritized your own kids and grandkids, ask Jesus to show you a person within your sphere of influence who is "fatherless" or "motherless." Ask God to show you how you can be a spiritual parent to this person. Discuss this insight with a prayer partner, or small group, then pray together:

Heavenly Father, do in my heart and life whatever you need to do for me to love this person like you have loved me. I know that any hope I have of showing others love, is because you have loved me first. Help me to accept any role you have for me as a "spiritual parent." Thank you for hearing my prayer and accomplishing your will in my life. I'm believing that you will accomplish this and have confidence in you.

 P10. A Spirit-empowered disciple consistently demonstrates love for Jesus by loving others at their point of need, knowing that it is really Jesus loving them.

Small Group: Week 4

On this day, we recommend that you spend some time sharing your responses with a spouse, friend, prayer partner, or small group. Reflect on your responses from previous days and then talk about them together:

I've spent some time with Jesus in prayer. He invited me to join him in loving _____ (name specific person) well. Because I love/care about him/her/you, I've asked the Lord to show me how to _____ (see response from Day 23 or share a new response).

In my prayer time recently, I asked God to show me things in my life that need to change, I sensed that God wants me to change my _____ and make me more _____ (affectionate, sensitive, patient, supportive, etc.). I'm committed to do that by _____ (see response from Day 24).

Think about your spouse/close friend/member of small group. What specific character qualities do you admire in him/her? What positive character traits have you noticed, and when have these traits been demonstrated? Finish this sentence and share it with each person of the group.

- *For example: I admire your enthusiasm. I see this quality in you when we work together in the yard. You are always excited to see the finished product and enjoy being outdoors.*

- *Or, I admire your patience. I see this quality in you when you talk about the difficult relationships at work.*

Here's a list of character qualities. Be ready to share one of these or one of your own:

• Boldness	• Generosity
• Compassion	• Gentleness
• Contentment	• Gratefulness
• Creativity	• Initiative
• Determination	• Integrity
• Diligence	• Loyalty
• Discernment	• Responsibility
• Endurance	• Sensitivity
• Fairness	• Sincerity
• Faith	• Understanding
• Flexibility	• Wisdom

I know God's Word tells me to make allowance for other's faults and to forgive as he has forgiven me, so I'm asking God to help me forgive because _____ (use no names as you share). I choose to forgive and make allowances because he has done the same for me (see response from Day 26).

As I live out my call to love, I would like to initiate a conversation with _____ and I plan to ask about _____ (see response from Day 22).

After I've listened to his/her story and found commonalities, I'll look for opportunities to share my story about _____ (see response from Day 22).

After we have progressed to a safe place in our relationship, I'll ask the Lord to lead me to share his story of saving power (see response from Day 22).

 **Encounter Jesus**

*But God showed his great love for us by sending Christ to die for us
while we were still sinners.*

ROMANS 5:8

*And when he comes, he will convict the world of its sin,
and of God's righteousness, and of the coming judgment.*

JOHN 16:8

As you complete this week of prayer moments, reflect again on Christ's call to love. Remember what Jesus has called us to and what he has not. Romans 5:8 reminds us that Jesus showed us his great love, even *while* we were sinners. He loves us despite our sinful behavior. And if John 13:34 tells us to love others, like we have been loved—it stands to reason that we too, are called to love people despite their sinful behavior.

But what about sin? Christ answers this himself. John 16:8 tells us that it is Christ's job to convict the world of sin. It is his role to give instructions for right living. Our job—our role—is simply to love.

Listen to Christ's words. Imagine him speaking directly to you:

> *I came to seek and to save you! I didn't wait until you shaped up or acted right. I loved you while you were imperfect and flawed. I looked beyond your faults and loved you while you were still a sinner. The world needs my kind of love; there's too much comparison, judgment, criticism, and self-righteousness. I am coming to convict the world of sin; I am the judge of righteousness. You look for opportunities to share how my love has changed you. Let me handle the rest.*

 M4. A Spirit-empowered disciple lives confidently that God is at work to convict others of sin, while encouraging others to please the Lord with their lives; being slow to blame others or to make them feel guilty.

Week 5

Love in the Household of Faith

As we embrace the love of Jesus, express our love for him, and live out our call to love the people nearest us, it's then time to prioritize our call to love other Jesus-followers.

The fourth circle is love expressed in the community of faith. This means that loving your church and other followers of Jesus is an expression of the depth of love you've experienced in the first three inner circles. A healthy disciple, with a healthy marriage and family, is able to effectively serve the local church as a servant leader by developing disciples who make disciples (John 13:34–35; 2 Timothy 2:2).

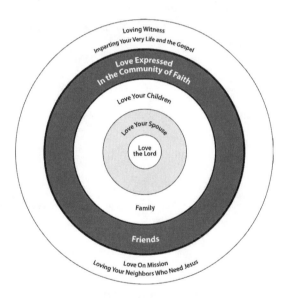

Therefore, whenever we have the opportunity,
we should do good to everyone—especially to those in the family of faith.
GALATIANS 6:10

Love as a Servant

To live out Jesus' call to love is to live as a servant—sharing his life, love, and the gospel.

Take a moment to remember a time when you were prompted to serve a friend, family member, or church member during a time of need. When did God involve you in ministry to another person at their point of need?

I recall when (who/what) _____ and God led me to _____.

- *For example: I recall a member of our church lost everything they owned during a fire. We arranged for food, clothing, and temporary housing; and supported them as they got back on their feet.*

Serving others with this kind of sensitivity and initiative is a critical part of loving like Jesus. Christ exemplified this when he noticed the many needs of hurting people around him and took initiative to meet those needs. Christ exemplified what it means to be a servant—and then calls us to do the same.

From *Love Like That*

by Les Parrott

Before the meal of bread and wine and Jesus' accompanying message of profound symbolism, he humbles himself in a way that shocked his disciples. He does something so incongruent to what they were expecting and so deeply meaningful that it was guaranteed to stick in their memory forever. Their teacher, their Lord, takes a towel and basin and begins carefully washing each man's feet with water. The disciples are stunned. Dismayed. Overwhelmed. This task was normally reserved for lowly servants. But here is their venerated rabbi kneeling before each of them, one after the other, to lovingly rinse the road dust from their feet.

It's an inversion. It's upside down and doesn't make sense. Power and recognition were on the minds of the disciples, and Jesus was demonstrating service and sacrifice. He knew each of them well: The boisterous James and John whom he called "sons of thunder," Simon the zealot whose passion for politics could be easily provoked, the skeptical Thomas who struggled with doubts, upbeat Andrew, rash-tongued Peter, and all the rest. Jesus even washed the feet of Judas whom he knew was about to betray him. Jesus looked each of these men in the eyes, considering their personalities, and displayed uncompromising humility. He didn't pay someone to wash their feet; Jesus did it himself. He became a lowly, unpretentious, self-giving servant.

It's easy to miss the profundity of this act because the gulf in time and culture between us and that fateful evening. A modern-day equivalent might be your pastor coming to your home to wash your dirty dishes or clean your bathrooms. Or maybe the governor of your state stopping by to sweep out your garage or separate your garbage.

The analogies lack the personal and intimate experience of what Jesus did, but they get at the startling act of humility and service. The self-giving act of their rabbi surely endeared the disciples to him more than ever.

Of course, what Jesus did was more than an act of affection. It's a life lesson. Jesus tells the disciples they must follow his example with each other. They must become like servants, setting aside concern for position and privilege. They must place others above themselves. Through foot washing, Jesus unforgettably showed that service, not status, is what he's about: "The Son of Man did not come to be served, but to serve."

 **Encounter Jesus**

"I have given you an example to follow. Do as I have done to you."
JOHN 13:15

Pause for a moment and imagine that Jesus is kneeling before you. Like he did with the disciples, the Savior has washed your feet. Listen as Jesus gently invites you to do the same:

I never consider you my servant, but I've called you to serve. Serve others like I serve and love you. The amazing thing is this: Any time you serve others and meet their needs, you are loving me. You honor me when you're generous, supportive, and kind. If you pour yourself out for others and satisfy the needs of the afflicted, I will bring special blessings to your life. Remember, others will know you're my followers when they see the Body of Christ loving one another.[3]

Tell Christ about your willingness to follow his example:

Jesus, I am grateful that you came to serve. You provide me with an amazing example of _____. Because you have loved and served me in such incredible ways, I want to do the same. I am committed to serving like you as I _____.

Even before that last night, Jesus spoke to his followers about this radical servant attitude. When they originally joined Jesus and his movement, three years earlier, they were focused on reaping rewards. They wanted a payoff for leaving their lives and following him. They quarreled over who would get what role. Two of them even had their mother make a special request to Jesus on their behalf, ensuring they'd be promoted. A constant power grab entwined the twelve.

Jesus told them repeatedly that power games were fundamentally alien to life inside God's kingdom. It's not about being first or more prominent. It's about heartfelt service. It's about love. But even up to the time of their final dinner together they were jockeying for position and squabbling over who was greatest. So Jesus leaves them—and us—with an indelible act that spoke in ways words cannot. He leaves us on the last night of his life with an unforgettable act of humble service summing up, perhaps more than anything else he did short of the cross, what it means to love like Jesus.

Just to be clear: Loving like Jesus is selfishness and self-focus in reverse. It is not concerned with benefits, and it expects nothing in return. Whether it is offering directions to someone who appears lost, giving an especially generous tip to a server who seems needy, or encouraging a friend who didn't get an expected promotion, self-giving love is done out of care, compassion, and kindness—expecting neither repayment or appreciation.

Loving like Jesus means offering the best of who you are to others, and it comes with no strings attached.

 **Experience Scripture**

> *"If I then, the Lord and the teacher, washed your feet,*
> *you also ought to wash one another's feet."*
> JOHN 13:14

Stop now and take notice of the opportunities within your church or community of believers. When might you express the love of Jesus to these fellow believers?

- Where are the unnoticed people around you? Start a conversation. Ask them about the details of their lives.

- Where are the people who need your support and helping hand? Offer to help a widow with her grocery shopping, help a young couple with childcare, or buy a cup of coffee for the church greeter who welcomes others with a smile.

- Where are the people who need encouragement or an uplifting demonstration of care? Take care packages to members who are in the hospital or volunteer to deliver meals to the elderly.

Follow Jesus' example and pray for the empowerment to live out this request:

Heavenly Father, I want to be a better servant to my family, friends and those in the household of faith. Help me lift my focus beyond myself to notice the needs of others. Holy Spirit, prompt my mind and empower my initiative to meet these needs.

 Engage with Your Community

So encourage each other and build each other up,
just as you are already doing.
1 THESSALONIANS 5:11

Discuss your plans with your spouse, friend, family member, or small group, then ask them to join you in executing your "love-like-Jesus plans." Invite this person to be a part of your plans. Together, offer the best of who you are—with no strings attached. With intentional humility and unselfishness, encourage one another to serve members of God's family.

 M9. A Spirit-empowered disciple consistently shares life and faith with friends and family; making disciples like Jesus did.

Make a Disciple

Our mission, which we call the Great Commission, was established with Christ's words on the Mount of Ascension: "'Therefore go and make disciples'" (Matthew 28:19–20 NIV). The Great Commission establishes the purpose for the church's existence: We are commissioned to worship the Lord with all we have, to win the lost, to train believers to become disciples, to use our ministry gifts, and to find environments of fellowship for connection.

What we often call the Great Commandment serves as a guide for how we go about this Great Commission. Jesus spelled out the Great Commandment, and love was front and center:

"'Love the Lord your God with all your heart and with all your soul and with all your mind.' This is the first and greatest commandment. And the second is like it: 'Love your neighbor as yourself.'"
MATTHEW 22:37–39 NIV

In light of our mission to make disciples, we can sometimes forget that love is to be the guiding force that governs how we pursue our mission. Paul admonishes us that without love—evidence of Spirit-empowerment—the rest is hollow and is nothing but a clanging cymbal, profiting us nothing. It's as vital to have love guiding our mission as it is to have the Holy Spirit empowering us to complete it.

Our mission is clear. Love is our guide. But what does it look like to make disciples through the lens of love?

From *A Spirit-Empowered Church*

by Alton Garrison

Spirit-empowered discipleship first requires a lifestyle of fresh encounters with Jesus. We must never get too busy working for him that we lose our relationship with him. Paul said, "I count all things to be loss in view of the surpassing value of knowing Christ Jesus my Lord" (Philippians 3:8 NASB). What kind of encounters with Jesus will mark the Spirit-empowered disciple? Here are just a few:

Jesus longs for our praise—praise from those he has blessed, healed, comforted, and encouraged. Therefore, one way to relate to Jesus is to reflect on his divine gifts and then give him praise. He is always comforting, always blessing, always encouraging, and always healing—but are we careful to give him praise?

Another way to have a productive encounter with Jesus is to be attentive to his voice—to listen to him. Many times, we think that to love Jesus and relate to him means that we get busy doing things for him. Jesus is longing for us to do just what Mary did—give him our undivided, focused attention. Luke wrote, "Mary ... sat at the Lord's feet and listened to his teaching" (Luke 10:39 ESV). If we get quiet, we'll hear him speak. His instructions never mislead us.

 Encounter Jesus

But all who listen to me will live in peace.
PROVERBS 1:33

Spend the next few moments living out this Bible verse; take this time to do the Book! Proverbs tells us that those who listen to the voice of wisdom live in peace. Jesus, our Wonderful Counselor, is our guide.

Imagine yourself sitting at the feet of Jesus. You see the kindness in his face and the warmth of his smile. He is ready to share these moments with you. Ask the Lord to speak to you and be ready to listen. Pray this kind of prayer:

Lord, as I seek to love others like you have loved me, would you show me the people whom you are calling me to serve? Who, in our church or community of faith needs more of your love demonstrated through me? Give me the peaceful reassurance that I am living out your calling and loving the way you love. Show me, Lord. I am listening ...

Quietly listen to the Lord until he reveals the person(s) who could benefit from more of his love. Listen with confidence because you can be certain that you are praying a prayer that is in accordance with his will. Make plans to serve the person(s) whom Jesus reveals are in need of your servant love:

I sense the Lord wants me to serve _____ by _____.

Secondly, to be a Spirit-empowered disciple, we need frequent experiences of Scriptures. We can't give out what we haven't received. If we love God, we'll love his Word. It's good to know doctrine and even to memorize the Bible, but it's more important to practice the Scriptures daily. That should be our goal.

Peter teaches us, "Since you have in obedience to the truth purified your souls for a sincere love of the brethren, fervently love one another from the heart" (1 Peter 1:22 NASB). Are we practicing that daily? We can practice it by rejoicing with a friend when they have received a great blessing or by comforting a person in their sorrow or by weeping "with those who weep" (Romans 12:15). This is "doing the Book"!

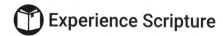 Experience Scripture

Weep with those who weep.
ROMANS 12:15B

Think again about the people around you who are struggling or in need. Who has a loved one who is ill? Who is struggling with their own health? Who is facing challenging circumstances with a teenager or aging parent? Who among your friends has lost their job or experienced the loss of infertility? Reflect on the friends, family, and members of the Body of Christ who are going through difficult circumstances.

Now plan your response as you "do the Book"! Live out and experience Romans 12:15b.

This passage of Scripture says that when another person is weeping, mourning, or feeling sad, our role is to weep with them. Contrary to our natural tendencies, our job is not to help them feel better. So, what does it sound like to experience Romans 12:15b? Here are some great ways to do the Book:

- *I am so sorry that you are going through this. It hurts my heart to know that _____.*

- *I'm saddened to hear that _____. Please know that I am praying for you.*

- *I feel a lot of compassion for you right now because _____. I am with you in all of this.*

- *My heart ached when I heard you say _____. You can count on my prayers and support.*

Plan a time to visit personally with the person who is struggling. Write a note or send a text that includes one of the responses above. Resist the tendency to give pep talks, advice, or spiritual platitudes. Just be with this person in their struggle. You want your friend or family member to know that they are not alone. This is what it looks like and sounds like to experience Romans 12:15b!

WE MUST SEE PEOPLE AS GOD SEES THEM OR WE WILL NEVER LOVE THEM AS HE LOVES THEM.

Finally, a Spirit-empowered lifestyle requires faithful engagement with God's people. But we must see people as both fallen and alone. They have spiritual needs as well as relational needs.

My friend, Dr. Ferguson, pointed something out in Scripture that I had never seen before—aloneness actually came before fallen-ness. In Genesis 2:18, God says that Adam was alone, and it was "not good." Several verses before Adam and Eve fell into sin (Genesis 3:6), God declared it was not good that Adam was alone. Ferguson observes, "Ministering acceptance and removing a person's aloneness does not mean that we condone sin. Rather, it means that we look deeper in order to see people's needs."

I'm convinced that the path to becoming a Spirit-empowered disciple begins with loving God and loving others, which we can't accomplish without the assistance of the Holy Spirit. A clear vision for discipleship means that virtually every church meeting or event must be designed to enhance relationships and equip people to love God with all their hearts, serve God gladly and effectively, and multiply themselves in the lives of others.

🧩 Engage with Your Community

One of the best ways to love like Jesus is to live out a Bible verse with them rather than quote the verse to them. Think of a person who doesn't know Jesus or is distant from God, but who has recently had a positive event occur in his or her life. Live out Romans 12:15a with this person. Be happy when they are happy—rejoice with those who rejoice. You'll be amazed at the connection that's built and the love they will experience as a result of this simple act.

Here's what your rejoicing or celebration could sound like:

After you've listened to and heard this person's life celebration, you might say:

• *I'm so excited for you! It's amazing to hear that _____.*

• *I'm happy for you. I'm glad to know that _____.*

• *Wow! How cool is that? It makes me smile to think about how much fun you had!*

 W1. A Spirit-empowered disciple falls in love with Jesus more and more because of consistent time spent in God's Word.

The Power of Acceptance

From *Relational Foundations*

by Great Commandment Network

Tears glistened in the eyes of Salvation Army officer Shaw as he looked at the three men before him. Shaw was a medical missionary who had just arrived in India, and the Army had been assigned to take over this colony of lepers. The three ailing men had their hands and feet bound with chains that cut into their diseased flesh.

Captain Shaw turned to the guard and said, "Please unfasten the chains."

"It isn't safe," the guard replied. "These men are dangerous criminals as well as lepers."

"I'll be responsible. They are suffering enough," Captain Shaw said. He put out his hand and took the keys, then knelt, tenderly removed the shackles, and treated the men's bleeding ankles and wrists.

Sometime later, Captain Shaw had his first misgivings about freeing the criminals. He had made plans for an overnight trip but dreaded leaving his wife and child alone. Shaw's wife insisted that she was not afraid, and that she felt secure in the care of the Almighty. When Mrs. Shaw went to the front door the following morning, she was startled to see the three criminals lying on her steps. One of the men explained in broken English, "We know the doctor go. We stay here all night, so no harm come to you."

This was how these "dangerous" men responded to an act of love. Captain Shaw saw the lepers through the compassionate, accepting eyes of Jesus. He did not see them as criminals, but as hurting, lonely men in need of comfort and friendship. One simple demonstration of acceptance brought gratitude to the hearts of men and glory to God.

The Power of Acceptance

Captain Shaw's testimony reminds us of the power of accepting one another as Christ has accepted us (Romans 15:7). If we hope to have a significant impact for the cause of Christ, we must begin to look for people who are failing and accept them with the grace of God. As we demonstrate the acceptance of Christ, our churches will become places of refuge, and those without a relationship with Christ will be compelled to know the one who empowers such grace.

We see evidence of the power of this relational apologetic in Jesus' interactions with the people of his day. Jesus demonstrated the life-changing results of acceptance when he encountered the woman at the well of Sychar (John 4:1–42).

In order to fully appreciate Christ's relational approach to faith, we must ask ourselves,

What was it about her dialogue with the Savior that prompted her to say, "Come, see a man who told me everything I ever did. Could this be the Christ" (v. 29)?

First, what do we know about this woman from reading this passage of Scripture and studying its context?

- From a Jewish perspective, this woman was an outcast, both because she was a Samaritan and because of her reputation in the community.

- This woman, by many accounts, had failed. She had been married five times, and the man with whom she was living at the time of her encounter with Jesus was not her husband (v. 18).

How did Christ demonstrate his acceptance of this woman?

- The woman must have been anticipating a very pious, unwelcoming response from Jesus. It was significant for a Jew to speak to a Samaritan. It was against social custom for a man to have a lengthy discussion with a woman in public. But it was unheard of for a Jewish teacher to speak to a Samaritan woman about issues of worship. Everything about Christ's discussion with this woman demonstrated His acceptance.

What impact did Christ's acceptance have on this woman and her community?

- The woman seemed convinced of the identity and deity of Christ, so much so that she invited others to meet him (v. 29). She was apparently so touched by the Savior's acceptance that she brought others to Jesus, eventually making a significant impact on her entire town (vv. 39-41).

What implications might the account of the woman at the well have for the twenty-first-century church?

As we demonstrate acceptance, others will be more receptive to the one who is the Source of this acceptance.

Since the woman was undoubtedly startled by the accepting love of Jesus, perhaps we should look for ways to startle others with the acceptance of Christ, while trusting the Holy Spirit to convict and make any needed changes.

There are certain members of the Christian community who are outspoken about specific groups of people, labeling them as "failures." Christ's acceptance should prompt a reevaluation of this approach and a reformation of heart for these members of the body of Christ.

Christ's ministry of acceptance made his rational arguments much more credible. Jesus did not stand at a distance and pronounce judgment, condemn, or ridicule. He took intentional initiative to show acceptance to the woman at the well. We can apply these same principles to our own lives and ministries.

Christ's ministry of acceptance was as much of an apologetic as any of the declarations He made about his identity. Could our lack of acceptance be part of the reason that so many unbelievers are taking no notice of what we have to say?

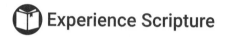 ## Experience Scripture

> *Therefore, accept each other just as Christ has accepted you*
> *so that God will be given glory.*
> ROMANS 15:7

Consider some of the following hindrances to showing acceptance to others. Which of these might be true for you? *I sometimes struggle with* _____ (such as):

- *being so busy with my agenda that I fail to notice people's needs.*

- *wanting to convince others of the truth of the Bible that I miss seeing their needs or point of view.*

- *thinking so much about people's spiritual needs that I overlook their relational or physical needs.*

- *not being able to see beyond a person's sin or the ways in which they are different from me. I am therefore not always sensitive to their need for acceptance.*

- *being judgmental, critical, or condemning.*

After you have identified your areas of hindrance, complete the following sentences:

I might sometimes struggle to accept others because I _____.

I regret this struggle or hindrance because I can see now that _____.

- For example: *I might sometimes struggle to accept others because I cannot see beyond a person's sin or the ways in which they are different from me. I regret this struggle because I can see now that even as I have prayed for several church members, my own lack of acceptance may have impacted their ability to receive God's truth.*

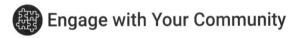 Engage with Your Community

Share your responses with a small group of friends. As you share, give accepting responses to one another. Such responses might sound like,

I can understand how hard that is for you, or *I am saddened to hear of your regret.*

As you share, keep in mind the promise of Romans 15:7: As we accept one another, thus expressing our gratitude for Christ's acceptance of us, praise is brought to God!

 Encounter Jesus

*Therefore, accept each other just as Christ has accepted you
so that God will be given glory.*
Romans 15:7

As a final step in this goal of accepting others, reflect for a moment on how Christ *has* accepted you.

- Has Jesus accepted you despite imperfections, shortcomings, weakness, and failures?
- Has Christ accepted you in the midst of wrong choices, selfishness, or pride?
- Has Christ accepted you before you changed or matured?

The answer to all these questions is yes. So thank Christ for his acceptance and then ask him to empower you to give the same. Pray and yield to the Spirit's work of perfecting your call to love like Jesus. Ask the Holy Spirit to help you embody the instruction of Romans 15:7. Pray that God would make the wonder of Christ's acceptance real in your life. Ask the Holy Spirit to enable you to demonstrate that acceptance to others in order to bring praise to God.

 P9. A Spirit-empowered disciple courageously serves others and lives out the love of Jesus with those who believe and with those who live differently.

The Power of Support

Have you ever felt beaten by the world?
Have you ever felt that your spirit had been stripped
and left bare to the harsh elements?
Have you ever felt that no one cares about your future?
I have been there.
I was the one lying on the side of the road as many passed by.
They continued on, unconcerned or unaware of my need.
But today I am thankful.
I'm thankful for the one who did stop and reach out.
I am grateful for the one who took the time
to bring comfort to my wounds;
thankful for the one who supported me
when I could not stand on my own.
I am grateful for the one who cared enough to see hope in my future.
I can share this story with you because of one …
one who became my neighbor and extended the love of God to me.
THE TRAVELER

From *Relational Foundations*

by Great Commandment Network

This beautiful poem, penned by an anonymous poet, captures the heart of one who has experienced the grace of God through the supportive care of another person. We can recall that the Good Samaritan provided practical and caring support to the traveler alongside the road, who was struggling to survive. Likewise, if we hope to restore relevance to our lives and ministries, every believer will have to become a "neighbor" to those outside of Christ and lavishly extend the love of God. In order to accomplish this relational apologetic, each of us must continue to look to Christ, reflecting on how he loved and then doing likewise.

The Power of Support

Christ continued to demonstrate a relational apologetic throughout the Gospels. Following the calming of the storm on the Sea of Galilee, the twelve disciples were more convinced than ever of the deity of Jesus. Christ's loving support during their time of struggle served as a compelling argument for faith in him (Matthew 8:23–27; Mark 4:35–41; Luke 8:22–25).

What do we learn about the disciples' encounter with the storm from reading this passage of Scripture and studying its context?

- Jesus and the disciples got into the boat to cross the Sea of Galilee. While Jesus slept, the disciples began to panic because of a storm that threatened their lives and safety. They awakened Jesus, and though he noted their limited faith, he ministered support to them. Christ spoke to the wind and the sea—and they were immediately calmed.

- The disciples were struggling with a physical force of nature; were possibly struggling against evil spirits; and were struggling to exercise faith in the words of God. Jesus had specifically told the disciples, "'Let us go over to the other side'" (Mark 4:35). His words were a promise that they were going to the other side!

What did Christ do that caused the disciples to ask (Matthew 8:27), "What kind of man is this?"

- Christ could have waited on the shore of Galilee as the disciples' faith was being tested. He could have watched from a distance as they fought against the storm. He could have left them alone in their struggle. But though he slept, Jesus was in the boat with the twelve. Though the disciples were filled with doubt, even to the point of questioning the Savior's care, Jesus showed his support. When his closest friends struggled to believe, Jesus got under the burden with them. He spoke to the wind and the waves—and the raging storm was stilled (Mark 4:39). In the aftermath of this powerful miracle, Christ was revealed as more than a great teacher; indeed, creation had obeyed its Creator!

 **Encounter Jesus**

There is no one like the God of Israel.
He rides across the heavens to help you,
across the skies in majestic splendor.
DEUTERONOMY 33:26

Reflect on some of the times when Jesus has supported you. Think about the times when you sensed that Jesus came to help, didn't leave you alone in a struggle and was very near to you during one of life's storms. Listen to the Savior's heart. Imagine that he is saying these words just to you:

Remember, there is nothing too hard for me. My power is unlimited. I'll ride across the heavens to help you—just call my name. And when you need to know how, or the load is too heavy, come to me. I'll be right there with you. I'm a gentle teacher and compassionate friend. Finally, I want you to know: It pleases me to give you strength. I love seeing how my strength enables you to do the work I've called you to do.[4]

Now respond to the Lord:

Jesus, I am grateful to you for the support I felt when _____.

It makes my heart feel _____ when I imagine that you are pleased when I ask for your help. I am _____ when I imagine you riding across the heavens to help me.

What implications might this account of the disciples' struggle have for us in our journey to love like Jesus?

- Just as Christ was with the disciples as they struggled against the storm, we will benefit from more intentional efforts to "be with" others as they encounter life's struggles. We must challenge ourselves to move away from a ministry mindset which invites unbelievers to "come and see" and replace it with one which compels us to "go and share." Relevance will be restored as we look for opportunities to join others in their burdens, reassuring them that they are not alone.

- Even though Jesus noted the disciples' lack of faith, he still offered supportive care. When we notice others, who have a lack of faith or stamina amid their struggles, we may pave the way for the good news of the gospel by "getting under the burden" with them. Countless people around us could be empowered to face their own personal struggles and responsibilities through our sharing of God's supportive love.

- Christ's demonstration of support gave testimony of his deity and solidified the disciples' belief in Him. As we support others during struggles with their marriage, children, health, and financial issues, the Lord will use those opportunities to reveal his care and draw others to himself. We need to open the eyes of our hearts to the countless people around us who are overcome by the cares of this life and feel that they are adrift on stormy seas.

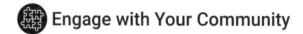 Engage with Your Community

If one part flourishes, every other part enters into the exuberance.
1 CORINTHIANS 12:25 MSG

As you reflect on your own salvation experience and your journey with the Lord, can you recall particular members of the body of Christ who were there to support you? Perhaps a friend has helped bear a burden or share a struggle. Was there a special family member who celebrated with you during a time of rejoicing? Was there someone who supported you during a time of struggle? Pause now and remember a time when the Lord provided his support through the care of another person.

I feel grateful as I remember how God brought _____ to support me when _____.

- For example: *I feel grateful as I remember how God brought two special friends to support me when I was having difficulties in my marriage. They cared for me when I felt completely alone and abandoned. I am not sure how I could have survived if they had not been around.*

- Or: *I feel grateful as I remember how God brought Gary to support me when I first became a follower of Christ. He helped me when I had so many questions about my faith. He was never impatient with me or judgmental concerning my struggles. He gently led me to the answers in God's Word.*

Share your responses with your spouse, friend, or small group. Rejoice with one another about God's provision of supportive care through his people. Your words of rejoicing might sound like,

- *I am thrilled to hear how God sent someone to support you in _____.*

- Or, *I am so glad that God sent someone to help you _____.*

- Or, *I rejoice with you over God's provision! He brought someone to _____.*

 Experience Scripture

Be generous with the different things God gave you,
passing them around so all get in on it.
1 Peter 4:10 MSG

Think about some of the "different things" God has given you and how you might more consistently offer your support.

- Has God given you time and extra patience? Could you offer to help a single mother in your church with childcare?

- Has God given you mechanical gifts and a heart to share goodness with others?

Could you begin a ministry to the widows of your church and provide car maintenance and repairs?

- Has God given you monetary resources and extra joy that can be shared with others? Could you give to a family who's struggling to meet expenses by providing a gift card for a local grocery store?

- Has God given you a gift of conversation and kindness? Could you serve the church as a greeter, host for newcomers, or welcome guests as they arrive in the parking lot?

Ask God to reveal the most meaningful ways you could support the household of faith.

God has given generously to me, so I plan to support _____ by _____.

P6. A Spirit-empowered disciple consistently shows love, joy, peace, patience, kindness, goodness, and self-control.

The Power of Comfort

Samantha's mother asked her to walk down the street to borrow a cup of sugar from a neighbor. Her mother was in a terrible hurry to finish a particular recipe, so she expected her daughter back in only a few minutes. After all, the neighbor lived only three houses down the street. Much to her mother's frustration, Samantha took much longer than expected to return home. Her mother was quite irritated and a little worried and demanded an explanation for her late arrival. Samantha explained that on her way home she met her friend, who lived next door. The friend was crying because her favorite baby doll had broken. "Oh," said the mother, "then you stopped to help her fix the doll?" "Oh, no," replied Samantha, "I stopped to help her cry."

Reaching a pain-filled world with the relevant message of the gospel requires the compassionate heart of the Savior. If we hope to reach others with the gospel, minister to those in the household of faith and live out our call to love, we will first have to move beyond our tendency to "fix" the world for Jesus—and, instead, stop to help people cry.

From *Relational Foundations*

by Great Commandment Network

The Power of Comfort

Jesus consistently demonstrated compassionate care as he encountered the lonely, hungry, tormented, and sorrowful. The Savior exemplified the power of a relational message that cares for those who are hurting and weeps for people who are in pain. Jesus' ministry to Mary and Martha at the tomb of Lazarus (John 11:17–44) is an especially poignant example to every believer of his commitment not just to "fix" the circumstances of our life, but to care for us in the midst of life's joys and sorrows.

When Jesus saw Mary weeping after her brother's death, Scripture tells us that, "He was deeply moved in spirit, and was troubled … Jesus wept" (vv. 33, 35 NASB). Lost and hurting people need the body of Christ to follow his example by noticing their pain and being deeply moved with compassion. They need us to care about their sorrows and weep because of their tears, thus living out the admonishment to "Mourn with those who mourn" (Romans 12:15).

What do we know about Mary and Martha and their encounter with Jesus at the tomb of Lazarus? What do we learn by reading this passage of Scripture and studying its context?

- Jesus could have come to Bethany much sooner, but chose to delay his arrival in order to bring praise and glory to God (John 11:1–15). Christ's subsequent testimony to the unbelievers was manifested both in the power of a God who can raise the dead, and in the compassion of a God who cries.

- Jesus had the power to save Lazarus without being physically present in Bethany. He could have given the command from afar and Lazarus would have been raised from the dead. But he chose to go to Bethany in order to be with Mary and Martha in their sorrow and comfort them in their pain.

- Christ's prayer to the Father revealed that he knew by faith that Lazarus would be raised from the dead. But in spite of the fact that Jesus knew the story would have a happy ending, he was moved with compassion because his friends were filled with sadness.

What did Christ's response communicate to Mary and to us?

- Just as Jesus hurt when he saw Mary's tears, he also hurts when he sees the sorrows of our lives. Our pain moves him with compassion (Psalm 103:13; 145:9).

What were the results of Christ's demonstration of compassion and care?

- The Savior's visible grief and tears of compassion communicated his love for Mary, Martha, and Lazarus. The crowd that watched his response that day was impacted by his love: "Then the Jews said, 'See how he loved him'" (v.36)! Jesus wept—and even the skeptics perceived it as an expression of his loving compassion.

- Many who witnessed the Savior's compassion and demonstration of power that day came to believe in him (v. 45).

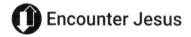 ## Encounter Jesus

Praise be to the God and Father of our Lord Jesus Christ, the Father of compassion and the God of all comfort, who comforts us in all our troubles, so that we can comfort those in any trouble with the comfort we ourselves have received from God.

2 CORINTHIANS 1:3–4

Take a moment and reflect on your own experiences and life events. Pause to recall a time when you felt some measure of sorrow, sadness, discouragement, or disappointment, and either no one knew, or no one was able to care for you. Can you remember a particular time of aloneness, either recently or in the distant past? Perhaps you experienced a tragic loss, significant betrayal, or painful rejection.

I remember a particular time of sadness/aloneness when _____.

- For example: *I remember a particular time of sadness/aloneness when our children had moved away from home and I realized that my husband and I did not know one another anymore.*

- For example: *I remember a particular time of sadness/aloneness when I was on a business trip and got the best news of my career—but there was no one around with whom I could celebrate. The joy of the moment was lost because I was alone.*

Now, reflect further on this occasion of aloneness. As you recall this time when you were saddened, disappointed, or discouraged, consider the Savior's heart for you at that moment. Could it be that during your time of sorrow, God was caring about your pain?

Pause to reflect on Jesus. Picture him before you, his heart moved with compassion for you just as it was for Mary in Bethany. Imagine the tear-filled eyes of Jesus as he sees you at your point of pain. The prophet Isaiah spoke of Israel's pain and affliction and declared, "In all their affliction He was afflicted" (Isaiah 63:9 NASB). Consider now that Christ was afflicted, sorrowed, and saddened as he looked compassionately upon you and your sorrow.

Imagine Christ's tender face and gentle embrace as he comes to you at your time of pain. He has made a special trip just to see you. His intent is to show you compassion and let you know he cares. Hear the words Christ speaks to you: *Precious child, my heart is sorrowed as I see you now. I am burdened by your pain and grieved by your loneliness. My heart is deeply moved for you. I am here for you, to love you and to reassure you that I care.*

Pause now and share with Christ what this truth does to your heart. Tell Him of your gratitude. Thank him for his comfort:

Dear Jesus, Thank you for your compassion. It means so much to me that _____.

I am so grateful that I have a God who hurts for me because _____.

 Experience Scripture

Praise be to the God and Father of our Lord Jesus Christ, the Father of compassion and the God of all comfort, who comforts us in all our troubles, so that we can comfort those in any trouble with the comfort we ourselves have received from God.

2 CORINTHIANS 1:3–4

Now that you have received comfort from Jesus, do what God's Word says: Comfort those who have experienced trouble with the same comfort you have received from God. Be imitators of the God of all comfort and comfort others just as Jesus has comforted you.

_____ *(name of the person) could benefit from some of the Lord's comfort delivered through me because they are going through* _____.

🧩 Engage with Your Community

Ask your spouse, prayer partner, or small group about their own experience of aloneness. Share your responses too. Allow the Holy Spirit to bring healing to your hearts as you mourn together and share the blessing of God's comfort.

Your words of comfort might sound like:

- *"I hurt for you because you have gone through such pain and felt so alone."*

- *"I care for you, and it saddens me that you have been alone in the midst of _____."*

As you finish sharing words of comfort, rejoice in the truth that you have imitated the God of all comfort and loved like Jesus. Rejoice in the blessing that can come when we mourn together and receive comfort.

> *God blesses those who mourn, for they will be comforted.*
> MATTHEW 5:4

 L10. A Spirit-empowered disciple becomes more and more like Jesus by imitating him and enjoying consistent times of being in His presence.

Be a Peacemaker

Racism is not just a socially taboo act that is hurtful to others; it is in direct violation of God. When we don't joyfully accept God's creation, we are not accepting him. Imagine being a parent and someone verbally or physically abuses your child due to who they are—too short, too tall, too outspoken, or too quiet. An involved and caring parent would be bothered by this injustice and feel that, not only was his child mistreated, but it was also a direct wrongdoing to the parent. Likewise, when we are not willing to fully accept and love others because they are different from us, we are directly hurting the heart of God.

From *The Ferguson Dilemma*

by Jade Lee

As a community, we are now faced with the challenges of overcoming the underlining issue of racism, but we do not always know how to change our views. Time and time again, it can seem as though racism is beginning to lose its hold, only for its unwelcomed grip to rise back into newspaper headlines, mirroring our darkened history.

Experiences such as isolation or mistreatment because of one's skin color can be very harmful. I cannot change the fact that I am a woman or a black woman. Color, like gender, is intrinsically related to identity. The scary reality is this sort of prejudice is easily denied by the others of another race. Like a cancer, it is unseen to the naked eye. Because society tends to see the material prior to seeing the immaterial, racial prejudice strongly affects one's psyche.

For example, the common saying, "Sticks and stones can break my bones, but words can never hurt me," although seemingly true, could not be further from the truth. Both words and thoughts can have drastic effects on the human soul. In talking to a sample of African American, African, and Caribbean youth between the ages of 19 and 25, they shared some racist experiences in their own lives, revealing that prejudiced words, thoughts, and actions can have long-term effects:

> When I was younger, I was constantly followed around stores when I walked in, especially [when I was] with other people. If I was with people of other races, they wouldn't follow them, just me or the other black people I was with (twenty-year-old African-American women).

In 8th grade when I moved to Georgia, I was walking to my friend's house and this group of white guys in a car screamed unidentifiable slurs and threw trash at me while they drove by. (Anonymous)

These statements bring clarification to what racism could look like in our current times. Oftentimes, in defining racism, it is easy to say, "I am not behaving or thinking that way. I can assure you, I'm not racist." But when seen from the other parties' perspective, our actions could be very harmful. Both overt and covert racism are present in the above stories.

Engage with Your Community

We will speak the truth in love.
EPHESIANS 4:15

Plan a time to talk with friends who have a different skin color, religious background, or cultural background than you. With gentleness and respect, speak the truth in love as you have the following conversations with them:

I have experienced racism and it has looked like/sounded like _____.

I want to be more sensitive and respectful to people of all races, so could you give me input about how to do that?

Jesus said it like this: "Truly I tell you, whatever you did for one of the least of these brothers and sisters of mine, you did for me … For I was hungry, and you gave me nothing to eat, I was thirsty and you gave me nothing to drink." This verse reveals Jesus' perspective on how we treat others. When we aim to restore relationship by uprooting racist thoughts, we are doing one of the most powerful and spiritual acts of love we could do for the children of God.

The good news is that no matter how many times I am talked down to or ignored, God teaches me new lessons in each painful moment. Others have come back to apologize, once realizing they made a judgment that was not based on truth. The black community has been through this sort of experience repeatedly and throughout generations. The white community is continuing to learn how to relate to a people that have *lived in* biased situations for many years.

But the battle is not hopeless. The more we listen for truth and are willing to let go of old thought patterns, we will begin to bridge the gaps that have caused ongoing misunderstanding. There is hope for a new beginning. If we remain committed to this process, together, we shall overcome.

> Racism springs from the lie that certain human beings are less than fully human. It's a self-centered falsehood that corrupts our minds into believing we are right to treat others as we would not want to be treated. (Alveda King)

A revival of relationships will begin in the home, in the community, in the church, and in the marketplace. This is what the soul of a broken nation is deeply longing for. We must all begin the work of introspection, acknowledging our own needs, asking God to come into our own heart so we can love as he loves. This unconditional love will break the chains unknowingly remaining in our hearts. It will tear down barriers that seemed impossible a moment before, enabling us to overcome years of deeply rooted hurt and pain.

 Encounter Jesus

> *But as he came closer to Jerusalem and saw the city ahead,*
> *he began to weep. "How I wish today that you of all people*
> *would understand the way to peace."*
> LUKE 19:41–42

Christ's reputation as a healer and teacher had spread throughout Galilee. So as he rode a small donkey down the winding trails, people began to recognize him. A crowd gathered and joyfully began to praise God. For the first time in ministry, Jesus was publicly praised. Then something odd occurred. He reached a certain point on the path to Jerusalem and began to cry. Cry? On a festive occasion such as this, what would prompt the Savior to cry?

Jesus *looked upon* Jerusalem—past her regal palace, past her standing as a strong military force and hub of commerce. Jesus looked past all that and saw the people. He came upon the city; saw the people's hurt—and his heart's response was to cry. What do you imagine Jesus sees and feels when he looks upon your community?

Because Jesus is the same yesterday, today, and forever, we can be confident that just as he felt compassion for Jerusalem, he feels compassion for us. The writer of Hebrews reminds us that

Jesus not only feels compassion for our needs, but he is in heaven, constantly interceding for us (Hebrews 7:25).

Picture this moment: Christ is praying for you, your marriage, your family, your church, and your community. He's praying with a heart of compassion. Picture Jesus leaning over and whispering a prayer to the Father. You overhear him praying for the needs of your life and community.

What does it do to your heart to know that Jesus loves you and the people around you so much that the needs of your lives move him with compassion—and that then, out of compassion, he intercedes for you?

Jesus, when I consider that you are praying for me because you feel compassion and care for me and my community, it brings _____ *to my heart.*

- For example: *joy, peace, gladness, thanks, awe, or wonder*

God's answer to a broken, divided people has been and will always be a Mediator. He has a bridge—a lawyer—who will bring the two parties back to the truth. This person will first bring them back to God, and then God will bring them to the place of reconciliation. As we see our wrong concepts, judgments, and prejudices, healing can begin.

Then we come back to God, apologizing for how we have viewed his creation. We ask for his perspective of the other party, which is many times different than our own. We humble ourselves as we see the greatest mediator of all—Jesus Christ—step in to heal all of our broken hearts.

 **Experience Scripture**

And those who are peacemakers will plant seeds of peace
and reap a harvest of righteousness.
JAMES 3:18

Ask the Lord to reveal opportunities where you could plant seeds of peace within relationships of your community. Plan to live out what God reveals. You might:

- Cultivate more friendships with people who are different from you.

- Take intentional steps to know and understand different cultural and racial tensions.

- Take initiative to cultivate racial and cultural diversity among your church's or community's leadership.

- Participate in events that highlight the priority of unity among races, cultures, and communities.

 P8. A Spirit-empowered disciple lives in peaceful relationships and works to help others live in God's peace as well.

Small Group: Week 5

On this day, we recommend that you spend some time sharing your responses with a spouse, friend, prayer partner, or small group. Reflect on your responses from previous days, and then talk about them together.

Live out Romans 12:15a with your spouse, friend, or small group. Be happy when they are happy—rejoice with those who rejoice. You'll be amazed at the connection that's built and the love you will experience as a result of this simple act (see Day 30).

One of the best memories/celebrations from my life is _____.

After you've listened to and heard each person's life celebration, you might say:

- *"I'm so excited for you! It's amazing to hear that _____."*

- *"I'm happy for you. I'm glad to know that _____."*

- *"Wow! How cool is that? It makes me smile to think about how much fun you had!"*

Live out Romans 12:15b with your spouse, friend, or small group: "Mourn with those who mourn." Ask each person to share the following and then live out the verse together:

- *One of the hardest memories/struggles from my life is _____.*

This passage of Scripture says that when another person is weeping, mourning, or feeling sad, our role is to weep with them. Contrary to our natural tendencies, our job is not to help them feel better. So, what does it sound like to experience Romans 12:15b? Here are some great ways to do the Book (see Day 30):

- *"I am so sorry that you are going through this. It hurts my heart to know that _____."*

- *"I'm saddened to hear that _____. Please know that I am praying for you."*

- *"I feel a lot of compassion for you right now because _____. I am with you in all of this."*

- *"My heart ached when I heard you say _____. You can count on my prayers and support."*

Consider some of the following hindrances to showing acceptance to others. Which of these might be true for you (see responses from Day 31)?

I sometimes struggle with ...

- *being so busy with my agenda that I fail to notice people's needs.*

- *wanting to convince others of the truth of the Bible that I miss seeing their needs or point of view.*

- *thinking so much about people's spiritual needs that I overlook their relational or physical needs.*

- *not being able to see beyond a person's sin or the ways in which they are different from me. I am therefore not always sensitive to their need for acceptance.*

- *being judgmental, critical, or condemning.*

After you have identified your areas of hindrance, complete the following sentences:

I might sometimes struggle to accept others because I _____.

I regret this struggle or hindrance because I can see now that _____ .

Ask God to reveal the most meaningful ways you could support the household of faith.

God has given generously to me, so I plan to support _____ by _____ (see response from Day 32).

 ## Experience Scripture

You are my refuge and my shield;
your word is my source of hope.
PSALM 119:14

Declare your absolute trust in God's Word, both to him and to his people. Close your time of sharing by completing the following:

God's Word is my source of hope because _____. *His Word has worked in my life when* _____.

I know the Bible is the answer to _____ *and he is my refuge and my shield as I* _____.

 W10. A Spirit-empowered disciple lives out an unwavering trust in God's Word—believing it is true, and trusting that it will never fail.

Week 6

Love on Mission

When we have experienced an abundant love with Jesus and have lived out our calling to love our nearest ones and members of the faith community, out of gratitude we'll be moved to share God's love on mission.

The outermost circle of a love like Jesus means imparting your life and the gospel. The apostle Paul modeled this in 1 Thessalonians 2:8 by saying, "We were well-pleased to impart to you not only the gospel of God but also our own lives" (NASB). As missional leaders empowered by the love of Christ, we can effectively lead the church to declare and demonstrate the gospel in the communities around us (1 Thessalonians 2:7–8; Acts 4:12).

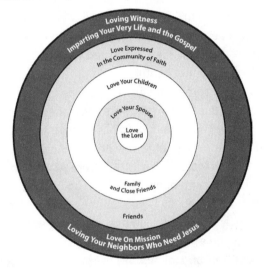

"Therefore, go and make disciples of all the nations, baptizing them in the name of the Father and the Son and the Holy Spirit. Teach these new disciples to obey all the commands I have given you. And be sure of this: I am with you always, even to the end of the age."
MATTHEW 28:19–20

Step toward Life Change

From *ReSet*

by Jeff Bogue

It was a huge crowd. The people were all waiting for someone to say something. So he stepped up and gave his first real sermon. It was a homerun! "Those who believed what Peter said were baptized and added to the church that day—about 3,000 in all" (Acts 2:41).

This was the real beginning of the church. On the day of Pentecost, the Holy Spirit filled the followers of Jesus and birthed a Jesus church movement that has lasted for more than two thousand years. It appears those early church leaders knew something about church growth that seems to elude most churches in the twenty-first century.

Today's church growth can sometimes be a mile wide and an inch deep. But the early church growth had spiritual depth because Jesus' followers had traded a legalistic religious theology for an experiential relational theology. These new Spirit-filled converts became committed disciples who shared an authentic and transformational faith with their neighbors and instilled that same faith into the next generation. Church historians say that from AD 100 to AD 300, the church exploded with spiritual growth, multiplying eight hundred times! That means, on average, the church quadrupled every generation for five consecutive generations. It grew from twenty-five thousand Christians in AD 100 to 20 million by AD 300! And in the process, they changed the known world!

The early Christians created a womblike atmosphere that was safe and conducive to answering questions, guiding discussion, and relationally being there for others to accept, encourage, support, and comfort. As a result, a sense of belonging and ownership was fostered, spiritual guidance was given and received, opportunities for service were seized, and accountability was accepted. "And each day the Lord added to their fellowship those who were being saved" (Acts 2:47).

When it comes down to it, this idea of transforming a dead person in sin into a brand-new person who can live forever is the stuff of miracles. It can't happen otherwise. Notice what the disciples asked when Jesus said it was nearly impossible for a rich man who relies on his own riches to make it to heaven: "'Then who in the world can be saved?'... Jesus looked at them intently and said, 'Humanly speaking, it is impossible. But with God everything is possible'" (Matthew 19:25–26).

That's really the point, isn't it? Jesus is either the miracle worker and our only hope, or he's not. He is either God and can forgive us because of his sacrificial death, or he isn't, and he can't. So, we all have a choice to make. To place our trust in Christ's death as our ransom out of slavery to sin and death requires that we make a choice to turn our backs on our self-effort and our self-reliant life and accept his miracle-working power to give us eternal life.

 **Encounter Jesus**

As each one has received a special gift, employ it in serving one another
as good stewards of the manifold grace of God.
1 PETER 4:10 NASB

Consider, for a moment, the manifold or "multifaceted" grace of God that you have received. If you have placed your trust in Christ's death as your ransom out of slavery to sin, then you have received eternal life. God's grace is also expressed toward you in other meaningful ways. These ways (or facets) of God's grace and love might look like:

- God has loved you by accepting you when you have failed (Romans 15:7).

- God has comforted you when you were sad, disappointed, or grieving (2 Corinthians 1:3–4).

- God has encouraged you when you were down (1 Thessalonians 5:11).

- God has supported you when you have struggled (Galatians 6:2).

Summarize one of your personal experiences of God's love and prepare to tell your story to someone who doesn't know Christ.

God gave me a personal gift of his love when _____. It was his love that made a huge difference in my life.

Talk about the ways that Jesus' grace changes your life. Your words might begin like this:

God's love is amazing because it changes me! God loved me even before I changed the way I _____. Because of his love, I now _____.

In the past, I tried to motivate people to trust in Christ out of fear. You know the drill: "If you want to avoid hell, turn to Jesus." But Jesus is not the great condemner; he is the great lover. And I began to see that if I could just help people grasp how much he loves them, they would repent of their self-effort and sin and turn to him. But, of course, that approach won't work unless and until we personally see just how much of a great lover God is.

I've found it is a mistake to rush or push people into a superficial prayer of forgiveness. It is better that they understand what Christ had to do and how he wants a relationship with them. Some time ago, I stopped asking people to pray a sinner's prayer until they really understood what they were repenting of. If the Holy Spirit isn't drawing a person to Jesus, and if that person doesn't see the need to repent, reciting a prayer isn't going to do much.

Leading people to Christ is really the role of a matchmaker. We merely introduce them to the one Person who wants an intimate love relationship for all eternity. God wants to reflect to seekers his love, kindness, and patience through matchmakers like you and me. I can *tell* people how much God loves them and wants a relationship with them, but my matchmaking will be much more effective if I am a living witness of that love. It is ultimately the Holy Spirit who must draw people to Jesus. And when the Holy Spirit is working through us—urging the seeker to respond to God's heart of love—that's when you and I can lead them to a relationship with Jesus.

 Experience Scripture

And then he told them,
"Go into all the world and preach the Good News to everyone."
MARK 16:15

Pause to ask God this question:

God, how could I better express your grace to others? What good news should I share about your love … to whom? How can I live out my call to love by sharing the good news with everyone?

I could share the good news of God's love with _____ by telling him/her about how God _____.

I will first ask about this person's story and listen to the challenges of their life. I plan to do that when _____.

I will demonstrate God's love by sharing my story, listening to his/her story and then telling about the Jesus story.

- For example: *I could share the good news of God's love with my boss, by telling him about how God is my Rock and source of strength. I will demonstrate God's love first by asking about the stress of the project at work and by listening to what he needs. My boss seems overwhelmed with all the demands at work, so I could possibly lighten his load by offering to help meet the deadline.*

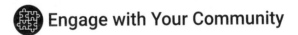 Engage with Your Community

*The earnest prayer of a righteous person has great power
and produces wonderful results.*
JAMES 5:16

Invite a friend, family member, or small group member to pray for you as you begin these spiritual conversations. Enlist support, encouragement, and wisdom from other members of the community of faith as needed.

 M8. A Spirit-empowered disciple actively engages in another's life story, so that a personal story of transformation can be shared, telling how Jesus has made a difference in life.

The Least of These

From *The Lamb's Agenda*

by Samuel Rodriguez

"Who do they believe I am?"
MATTHEW 16:13 TPT

This biblical passage captures one of the most transformative moments in human history. Peter revealed Jesus. Jesus revealed the church, activated divine purpose, and emancipated the kingdom. Revelation always leads to activation, and activation always leads to emancipation. We need a revelation of Jesus to activate the church's purpose, as we lead a movement of righteousness and justice. We need a movement of the Lamb's agenda … and the Lamb's agenda is nothing other than the agenda of Christ.

The agenda of Christ is drawn from the cross of Christ. And the cross of Christ is both vertical and horizontal. Vertically, we stand connected to God, his kingdom, eternal life, divine principles, and glory. Horizontally—to our left and to our right—we exist surrounded by and revealed through relationships, family, and community. Jesus' model of ministry was revolutionary. He embraced the banished, forgave those tormented by guilt, liberated those oppressed by evil spirits, and fed the hungry. His life was the cross in action—both planes of it—vertical and horizontal.

In the same way, our vertical salvation must lead to horizontal transformation. The good news must not only be preached, it must also be lived out. So how do we live out the Lamb's agenda? We read Matthew 25 and we heed it. We read John 3:16 and acknowledge it. We cannot easily justify a Christian ministry that convenes on Sunday morning and ignores its community from Monday through Saturday. Nor can we easily justify a ministry that treats Sunday like just another day to "do good" in the community. We derive our influence in that community, not from our ability to plan events and schedule speakers, not from our eagerness to distribute food and fix houses. We derive our influence from our source of enlightenment and our willingness to share that light with those around us. The good we do in the community must flow from a power beyond us. Governments can give out more food than we can, and celebrities can draw more people, but only we can share the light of God in every good deed we do.

 Encounter with Jesus

But God demonstrates his own love toward us,
in that while we were yet sinners, Christ died for us.
ROMANS 5:8 NASB

Reflect on the scene from Calvary. Remember what Jesus did ... and that he did it for you. He took your punishment; he gave his life to save yours. Share with him your gratitude for the cross:

Jesus, I don't want to ever get over the miracle and wonder of the cross. So thank you for

_____.

Next, allow your heart to consider this question: What if I could give back to Jesus? He did so much for me—what if there was some way I could "return the love"?

Miraculously, you can! Imagine the scene from the poorest parts of your city. Imagine the people who line the streets asking for food or money, with their torn clothes and unkempt hair. Reflect on the often-invisible faces that are worn from exposure to the elements. And now imagine that Jesus stands on those same street corners and he makes this declaration:

"When you did it to one of the least of these my brothers and sisters,
you were doing it to me!"
MATTHEW 25:40

Ask the Holy Spirit to speak to you about ways you could more effectively give to the least of these—and all the while express your love to him:

Jesus, am I doing all that you desire when I see the homeless in my community? I want to see your face on those street corners. Help me give to the least of these, as an expression of my love to you.

A Matthew 25 Movement

There's work to be done when thirty million people live in poverty. So where do we turn for answers? We turn to the Lamb and his agenda. You see the Lamb's agenda reconciles the sanctification and covenant of John 3:16 with the service and community of Matthew 25. There is a necessary link between compassion and evangelism. Each loses value without the other. Therefore, any church or Christian ignoring the plight of their neighbors lives an incomplete gospel.

Are we anointed to build great cathedrals or multimillion-dollar ministry platforms? Are we anointed to gather thousands around us to make them feel good about themselves and give them some place to go on Sunday mornings before brunch? I don't think so. We are anointed to bring good news to the poor, freedom to the captive, and healing to the brokenhearted.

In Matthew 25, Christ admonishes us to feed the hungry and clothe the needy. Yet today, unfortunately, American Christendom too often measures success by the metrics of rows filled, books sold, and dollars collected rather than by the number of souls transformed. To recalculate our metrics, we need to ask ourselves, *How does God measure success?*

The answer is simple and can be found in Matthew 25:34–36: "Come, you who are blessed by my Father, inherit the Kingdom prepared for you from the creation of the world. I was hungry, and you fed me. I was thirsty, and you gave me a drink. I was a stranger, and you invited me into your home."

 **Experience Scripture**

Real religion, the kind that passes muster before God the Father, is this: Reach out to the homeless and loveless in their plight, and guard against corruption from the godless world.
JAMES 1:27 MSG

Do a quick assessment of your own ministry to the "least of these." How are you making a difference in the lives of those who are hungry, homeless, or needy? God has called us to love—and from his perspective, we are most like him when we are loving people in need.

As I look at my personal effort to minister to the vulnerable, needy, or homeless, I realize that I _____.

I could do a better job of ministering to the least of these by _____.

Finally, the good news is that God is pouring out a fresh anointing upon a generation. God is anointing a generation that will deliver our brothers and sisters from malnourishment and hunger, as well as from physical and spiritual poverty. He is anointing a generation to knock down the walls of racial and economic injustice.

With this agenda—the Lamb's agenda—the church can address the social, spiritual, physical, intellectual, and communal needs of all its constituents. To do so, it must reconcile the vertical and horizontal planes of the cross. [The church] must be committed to the nexus of the cross.

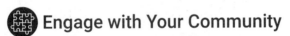 Engage with Your Community

In the same way, he will provide and increase your resources
and then produce a great harvest of generosity in you.
2 CORINTHIANS 9:10

If you are not already involved with a ministry to the homeless or needy in your community, do some research about the organizations that serve these needs. Ask how you can contribute. Volunteer—give your time, talents, and/or monetary gifts in order to minister to "the least of these." Look for ways to generously give and live out your call to love.

Finally, claim the promise of 2 Corinthians 9:10. Declare your faith in God, looking for ways that he provides for you and increases your resources so that you are be better equipped to be generous with others.

 M5. A Spirit-empowered disciple pursues opportunities to share, serve, and help others who are in need in local communities and around the world.

Turning a Nation to God

From *America*

by Tony Evans

The American dream is quickly becoming the American nightmare as more and more citizens become disillusioned with the direction things seem to be going. The constant threat of terrorism and an overblown debt threaten not only our economic future, but the future of our children and grandchildren as well. And as people gather unofficially around the water cooler at work—or officially around government-sanctioned summits, seeking to find solutions to the myriad of issues that plague us—real long-term answers continue to elude us.

There are only two explanations before us as we witness what is happening to our beloved nation. Either we are on the verge of the completion of an eschatology calendar that will usher in the return of Christ to judge the earth and set up his earthly kingdom, or we are enduring the passive wrath of God whereby he allows a person or a society to experience the consequences of their rejection of him. The more people marginalize the true God of the Bible the more chaotic things become.

However, such judgment opens the door for revival when God's church returns to him in humility and repentance. The return of Christ is outside of our hands, but revival and its social and cultural benefits are very much in our hands. Even when the church has become an unintentional co-conspirator in the culture's demise through its compromise with the culture, it can be empowered when it turns about to God in repentance.

This is a call for America to turn to God in hopes that he will reverse our course and restore our union to his definition of what a nation is to be when it operates under his rule. Such a restoration must be led by his church; for God will not skip the church house in order to change the White House (Ephesians 3:10).

God and his rule are America's only hope; and the church operating under his authority is the means for the realization of that hope, since it alone has been given the keys of the kingdom (Matthew 16:18–19). It is my prayer that God will use this movement to encourage, inspire, and challenge believers in Christ to become kingdom disciples through whom our God can work to bring revival to his church and, through it, to our land.

A Declaration of Dependence

Since national revival begins with Christians comprehensively functioning under God's rule, it is past time for a new declaration. America was born out of a desire for independence from the tyranny of England. But spiritual revival demands just the opposite: It requires verbal and visible dependence on God.

IF WE WANT GOD TO BLESS AMERICA,
THEN AMERICA MUST FIRST BLESS GOD.

This means his people must first totally dedicate allegiance to him through the four covenantal kingdom spheres he has established. Those four spheres are personal, familial, church, and national.

A personal declaration of dependence

Every Christian must decide to no longer serve two masters. God makes it clear that we cannot have the world and have him at the same time (1 John 2:15–17). Practically, this means that God's person, principles, and precepts must be brought to bear on all our decisions (not just the so-called religious ones). He must be Lord of all of life. Each day must begin with a commitment to him above all else, and he is to be consulted in prayer on all matters of life (Luke 9:23).

A family declaration of dependence

Heads of households must make the declaration of Joshua the slogan for their own home: "'As for me and my house, we will serve the LORD'" (Joshua 24:15 [ESV]). The dinner table must again become the central place for reviewing and applying kingdom principles (Psalm 128:3). Couples must reconnect themselves to their biblical roles and hate divorce as much as God does (Malachi 2:14). There must be a regular review of the progress the family is making at adhering to godly principles, and the family altar must become central in the home.

The church's declaration of dependence

Local churches must recommit themselves to their primary responsibility of making disciples and not be satisfied with simply expanding their membership.

JESUS DOESN'T NEED MORE FANS.
HE WANTS MORE FOLLOWERS.

Programs must be evaluated in terms of whether they are growing visible, verbal followers of Christ and not by how many people are entertained by church events. This means that there must be loving accountability incorporated into the life of the church. In addition, there must be a radical return by church leadership to the authority of Scripture and the priority of prayer as the foundation of church life (1 Timothy 2:8–9). The church must have regular, unified sacred gatherings to keep the focus on our absolute dependency on God.

A national declaration of dependence

The church must again become the conscience of the government. Through its national solemn assembly, it should clearly and respectfully call political leaders to God's principles for government (Romans 13:1–7), which means we cannot be so entrenched with political parties that we are not free to speak truth to power. It also means we must begin speaking with one voice, so the nation sees a unified church and not one divided by faith (Ephesians 4:13). In addition, we should so overwhelm the culture with good works that the benefit we bring cannot be overlooked or denied (Matthew 5:16). Finally, all attempts to remove God from the marketplace ought to be resisted while we simultaneously bring our public officials in prayer before the throne of grace (1 Timothy 2:1–3).

As God's kingdom agenda is manifested simultaneously through his four covenantal spheres in a spirit of dependence on him, then we will have done our part in welcoming the glory of our great God to be.

 **Encounter Jesus**

Christ in you, the hope of glory.
COLOSSIANS 1:27 NASB

Consider for a moment how God sees you as a bearer of his glory for your family, friends, community, and nation. Since he has placed the Spirit of the living God within the heart of every believer, we *are* the hope of his glory being revealed to the world around us. Because Christ is in you, you are the hope of his glory!

How does this impact your heart?

When I reflect on the truth that Christ is in me and I get to reveal his glory, I feel _____.

 Engage with Your Community

Plan to share your reflections with a friend, family member, or small group:

I want to do my part to reveal God's glory—to show the incredible power of Jesus Christ in the world in which I live. He's recently shown me how I need to change _____ so that I can be a better representation of Him.

Experience Scripture

"'In the same way, let your good deeds shine out for all to see, so that everyone will praise your Heavenly Father.'"
MATTHEW 5:16

Ask the Holy Spirit to show you ways in which you can reach out and do your part to overwhelm your community with good works. How will you serve your neighbors so that your good deeds will shine for all to see?

Holy Spirit, show me how I can "do good" for the people in my community who need it the most. Give me creative ideas and practical applications for how to best love the people you have placed around me. Help me to point others to you as I serve them with the love you have poured into my heart.

 P2. A Spirit-empowered disciple regularly looks for ways to share God's love with people in startling ways—spontaneously giving without any expectation of return.

What Does It Look Like to Love Your City?

From *Unlikely: Setting Aside Our Differences to Live Out the Gospel*

by Kevin Palau

How much do you love your city or town? Are you proud of it? What does it even mean to love your city? How can you get your arms around something so immense and complicated? Is it just wearing your Detroit Lions, Brooklyn Nets, or Columbus Crew jersey?

Over the years, I've been part of amazing prayer efforts to seek God on behalf of our community. Prayer is a given. It's where we begin. It's where we strengthen our efforts, and it's where we constantly return when we need to revive our hearts. The question is, where do we go from there? How and why do we love our city?

Those destined to be kings are those who know how to love. And Jesus lived the model. He practiced what He preached. Jesus bent down to wash His disciples' feet. In those days, washing feet was one of the lowest jobs—when everyone walked around on dirty roads in sandals with sheep dung and dirt and grime between their toes. The king of all the earth took on the lowest job for Himself—ultimately going to the cross to atone for the dirt, grime, and dung of our sin, washing and cleansing us, reconciling us to God.

God is a servant. And the gospel says when we serve, there's something that happens inside of us. When we stretch ourselves to share the Good News, we grow. There's a formation that occurs: we are formed, we are changed. We are shaped into the image of Jesus. As the body of Christ, propelled by His Spirit of love, we are a community of servants. This isn't just a project; this is what we do. This is who we are. We serve to follow in the dust of Jesus, our Great Servant, the One who has served us.

I'm convinced that to see greater impact in our cities we need to act on our prayers, step out of ourselves, and think smaller—much smaller. There are many stories about wide-sweeping city movements—efforts that span communities and include dozens, if not hundreds of churches. I love to see that kind of kingdom impact. But we can't forget where this all starts. It starts with individuals who are digging deep into their own neighborhoods or parishes, and who are expressing the gospel to family and friends through their words, their actions, and their motives.

 Encounter Jesus

But among you it will be different. Those who are the greatest among you should take the lowest rank, and the leader should be like a servant. Who is more important, the one who sits at the table or the one who serves? The one who sits at the table, of course. But not here! For I am among you as one who serves.

LUKE 22:26-28

Ask the Holy Spirit to reveal more and more about the character of Jesus and how he has served you with his love. Does the Spirit want you to remember that Jesus is the All-Powerful One, the Mighty Counselor, the Great I Am, the Prince of Peace, the Great Provider, the Attentive One, the Gracious One, or the Great Physician? One of the Spirit's jobs is to reveal more of Jesus so ask him to speak.

Holy Spirit, what do You want me to remember about Jesus and his servant-hearted love for me? What do You want me to know about Him? Listen as the Spirit testifies more about Jesus.

Next, ask the Spirit to reveal one of the ways he might want to you be different—how he wants to make you more of a servant so that you might look more like Jesus.

Holy Spirit, what changes do you want to make in me so I can serve more people with your love?

 Experience Scripture

Has the Lord redeemed you? Then speak out! Tell others he has redeemed you from your enemies.

PSALM 107:2

Ask the Spirit to remind you of a time when he was hoping you would speak out about the ways he has redeemed you. Ask the Spirit to bring to mind some of the times when he wanted to you to share the ways Jesus has changed your life, but you missed the opportunity.

Lord, speak to me about a time when you were hoping I would speak out about the ways you have redeemed me and loved me. I could have shared more with _____, but I missed the opportunity. I could have talked to _____ but I didn't.

As the Holy Spirit speaks to you, offer a humble prayer.

Lord, I want the boldness to speak out! I want to tell others in my city how you have redeemed me. I regret the times when I have missed your prompting. Make me more sensitive to your voice and give me the power to tell what you have done.

For most of us, we can easily get lost in the complexity of the greater whole of our city or town, but when we stop to think and dream about our little corner of the city, we can incite great change—both now and for eternity. That's one of the beauties of the body of Christ. We're universal and quite large, and yet we're small and compact. To see greater impact in our cities, we need to act on our prayers, step out of ourselves, and think smaller—much smaller.

The church, collectively, is frequently the only institution in any given city or region dispersed into every nook and cranny. Christians work and live in every walk of life, every vocation, and at every level of education, and, therefore, the church permeates all sectors of culture. When we cease viewing the church as a building of some sort and instead see it for what it truly is—the children of God who gather to worship Him and serve—we begin to see that not even Starbucks or McDonald's has this sort of market penetration!

You want grassroots? What is more grassroots than the church? And the funny thing is, those outside the church often get this better than we do. Now that we see the potential reach, you and I represent in culture, let's ask the question again: What does it look like to love your city?

Engage in Community

Where the Spirit of the Lord is there is liberty.
2 Corinthians 3:17

Talk and pray with a partner or small group about the practical ways the Lord might want you to love your city well. Ask for the Spirit's freedom and liberty to think, plan and creatively identify how you can be a part of sharing Christ's love to those in your little corner of your city.

Jesus, I invite you to open my mind, my heart and my perspective. Give me liberty to see new and effective ways we can love our city well.

 W3. A Spirit-empowered disciple consistently obeys God's Word and allows it to bring change, in order to be more like Jesus.

Live Compelled by Love

From *Compelled by Love*

by Ed Stetzer and Philip Nation

Luke 15:1–7, about the one lost sheep, is the first portion of perhaps the most well-known parable in the Gospels. For those who grew up going to church, it conjures up memories of flannel board pictures and spontaneous dramas led by Sunday School teachers. But do not be fooled. It is a story about the very nature of God and the heart of His church. It is revolutionary—and offensive to many.

In the context of the passage, we hear the Pharisees' words, dripping with sarcasm about Christ's fraternizing with "sinners." They were scandalized by whom he regarded as his friends.

Two thousand years later, we still have that problem. Do we want to do ministry on "that side of town?" Should we really let "those teenagers" go on the retreat? It seems we work hard to insulate ourselves from the very world Jesus says we should be focused on. We have successfully created, without malicious design, a Christian bubble—an evangelical subculture—where Christians live surrounded only by other Christians, and as a result, there are few among the lost whom we get to know intimately.

Christian experts tell us how to raise our kids, how to handle our finances, what music to buy, what movies to see, and which books to read. The bubble is complete. But God is on a mission outside that bubble.

In God, we find the Father, Son, and Spirit who intentionally search for the lost. God purposely goes to those who are far from him (that's us). He is fully aware of humankind's fall, yet isn't afraid to get his hands dirty. God seeks the lost, and we—in our missional assignment—are to do the same.

In the Luke 15 parable, the shepherd has 99 of his 100 sheep. I suspect many bosses would be happy if an employee had a 99 percent success rate. If you had a year with 99 percent success, the result would be praise, pay raises, promotions, and recognition at the annual retreat—because, after all, no one can get it right 100 percent of the time. Right?

The Father stands such conventional wisdom on its head. For the Father, if one sheep is lost, he keeps searching "until …." He doesn't give up. His searching is an "until found" search, not "until tired." It is "until rescued," not "until obligations are fulfilled." It is "until redeemed," not "until conscience is alleviated." God's searching love is one that ends in joy. Too often we seek only a sense of relief.

Love Brings Back the Strays

The Father responds differently [from us] when he rescues a stray. He lays the lost lamb across his shoulders. Great care is taken of the lost one. God says, "'I will seek the lost, bring back the strays, bandage the injured, and strengthen the weak, but I will destroy the fat and the strong. I will shepherd them with justice'" (Ezekiel 34:16 [CSB]). It isn't a "get-the-job-done" attitude. Someone is lost—wandering off the path by accident; others are strays—intentionally leaving the path in rebellion. Never minding the reason, the Great Shepherd searches for the lamb, bandages its wounds, and works justly.

When Ezekiel wrote this passage, Israel had been disobeying God's command to care for the poor and oppressed. Selfishness overrode the ethic Yahweh had given them. Ezekiel proclaimed that God is seeking strays—the very sheep that were causing a problem.

It's the pet you don't want to chase down the road, the child who continually frustrates you, or the person you see in the mirror every day (because you know your own sin). But God goes searching, even for the most frustrating strays.

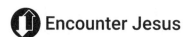 **Encounter Jesus**

"'For the Son of Man came to seek and save those who are lost.'"
LUKE 19:10

Listen to the words of Jesus. Imagine Him speaking directly to you:

> *I came to seek and to save you! I didn't want to experience heaven without you, so I took initiative to save you and call you to myself. And just like the Father sent me, I am sending you. Tell people about the great things the Father has in store for those who believe. Let's celebrate our love for Him and for one another so often that you can be the first to raise your hand and say, "Here I am, Lord—send me!"[5]*

Now, respond to the Lord in prayer:

Jesus, I am grateful you came to find me and save me. I am especially grateful because _____.

Lord, remind me often of how you came to save me despite my flaws and frustrations. Give me divine boldness, courage, and grace to do the same.

Love Heals the Wounded

The Father does not search just so he can be proud of maintaining a 100 percent record. Rather, his searching love is focused on the goal of healing the wounded. When you search for a believer gone astray, you are working alongside God himself. In the middle of proclaiming the gospel to a lost soul, God is pleading his case through you by his loving heart. As you quietly discuss the claims of Christ with someone "far from God," the Father is planting seed in soil he has already tilled. Even if you give up and leave, he is still at work in that life. The Father's searching love is boundless compared to ours.

Our agenda should change. We have a directive from the Lord to not give up on the people around us. He lovingly and persistently pursues them—and we walk with Him in that pursuit.

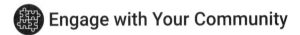 **Engage with Your Community**

Therefore, accept each other just as Christ has accepted you so that God will be given glory.
ROMANS 15:7

Recall a time when someone looked beyond your faults and saw your needs. When did you receive some of Christ's unconditional love despite your behavior? Plan to share this memory with another person. Recount both your experience and your feelings related to the unconditional love you received:

Someone looked past my behavior and showed me grace when _____. And, as a result, I remember feeling so grateful because _____.

Ask the Holy Spirit to give you the opportunity to share some of God's unconditional love with someone around you:

Lord, show me another person whose behavior is less than perfect—but then give me the opportunity to share some of your unconditional love with them.

Your responses might sound like this:

- *I know that time must have been so hard for you.*

- *I am sad that you experienced those difficult things.*

- *Thanks for telling me about the hard places of your life. We all struggle in some way, don't we?*

 Experience Scripture

So we are Christ's ambassadors; God is making his appeal through us.
2 CORINTHIANS 5:20

Ask the Holy Spirit to show you what might be hindering you from more effective ministry outside the "Christian bubble." What keeps you from your missional assignments as God's ambassador? Could it be …

- a matter of wrong priorities?

- a struggle with materialism?

- fearful anxiety?

- concerns about receiving others' approval?

- over-attention to activity or achievement?

- or preoccupation with your own plans and goals?

Lord, show me what keeps me from becoming more of an ambassador for you.

Quiet your heart and listen until you sense an answer from the Lord. Then complete the following sentence:

My ministry as an ambassador for Christ might, at times, be hindered by _____.

Finally, invite your spouse, friend, or small group to encourage you to live on mission. Plan to share your responses above with this other person. Then take some time to pray together, asking God to remove these hindrances and empower your change. Ask them to pray with you about your calling to live out the Great Commission and fulfill God's call to love.

 M3. A Spirit-empowered disciple lives with confidence that Jesus is the only hope we have for a life in heaven and a life of joy here on earth.

About the Authors
and Their Resources

MARK BATTERSON

Excerpt from: *Wild Goose Chase: Reclaim the Adventure of Pursuing God*
Copyright © 2008 by Mark Batterson
Publisher: WaterBrook Multnomah—an imprint of Random House, a division of Penguin Random House LLC. All rights reserved.
ISBN: 978-1-5905-2719-1

About the Author:

Mark Batterson is the New York Times bestselling author of *The Circle Maker*, *The Grave Robber*, and *A Trip around the Sun*. He is the lead pastor of National Community Church—one church with seven campuses in Washington, DC. Mark has a doctor of ministry degree from Regent University and lives on Capitol Hill with his wife, Lora, and their three children. Learn more at www.markbatterson.com.

JEFFREY A. BOGUE

Excerpt from: *ReSet: Why Discipleship Isn't about Trying Harder*
Copyright © 2013 by Jeffrey A. Bogue
Publisher: Living Naked Press
ISBN: 978-1-6289-0518-2

About the Author:

Jeff Bogue serves as senior pastor for Grace Church in Akron, Ohio. Jeff, his wife Heidi, and their ministry team lead multiple campuses and church plants with over ten thousand people calling Grace their home. Jeff's story isn't about his pastoral skills or leadership; it's about his struggles to overcome his misconceptions of God, himself, and his role in discipling people to maturity in Christ. You will find his story inspiring, challenging, and instructional in raising up committed followers of Jesus through the relational heart of God. Dr. Bogue and his wife, Heidi, have been married twenty-six years and have six children. To purchase this complete book, go to https://store.graceohio.org.

GARY CHAPMAN

Excerpt from: *Loving Your Spouse When You Feel Like Walking Away*
Copyright © 2008, 2018 Marriage and Family Life Consultants, Inc.
Publisher: Northfield Publishing
ISBN: 978-0-8024-1810-4

About the Author:

Gary Chapman—author, speaker, and counselor—has a passion for people and for helping them form lasting relationships. He is the bestselling author of *The 5 Love Languages*® series and is the director of Marriage and Family Life Consultants, Inc. Gary travels the world presenting seminars, and his radio programs air on more than four hundred stations. For more information, visit 5love-languages.com.

DARRYL DELHOUSAYE

Excerpt from: *The Primacy of Our Faith*
Copyright © 2017 Darryl DelHousaye
Publisher: LLJ Ministries, LLC
ISBN: 978-1-5413-5091-5

About the Author:

Darryl DelHousaye draws on a lifetime of ministry experience and deep study of Scripture to bring his unique insights on God's plan and purpose for the church and for the world. Darryl began his ministerial experience as a pastor in California at Grace Community Church in Sun Valley and First Baptist Church in San Lorenzo Valley. He then moved to Arizona where he was senior pastor at Scottsdale Bible Church for twenty-five years. For the past twenty years, Darryl has been President and Professor of Pastoral Theology at Phoenix seminary. As a nationally recognized Bible teacher and theologian, Darryl maintains a rigorous schedule of preaching and teaching. To purchase the full resource, go to amazon.com.

JONI EARECKSON TADA

Excerpt from: *The God I Love: A Lifetime of Walking with Jesus*
Copyright © 2003 Joni Eareckson Tada
Publisher: Zondervan
ISBN: 978-0-3102-4008-2

About the Author:

Joni Eareckson Tada, the Founder and CEO of Joni and Friends International Disability Center, is an international advocate for people with disabilities. Her newest book, *A Spectacle of Glory*, won best devotional book in the Evangelical Christian Publishers Association's 2017 Christian Book Awards—it contains fresh biblical insights from her battle with chronic pain. Her book *A Step Further* won the

Gold Medallion Award. Joni is General Editor of Tyndale's *Beyond Suffering Bible*—a special edition published for those who suffer chronic conditions, and their caregivers. She and her husband Ken were married in 1982 and reside in Calabasas, California. You can learn more about Joni's ministry at www.joniandfriends.org.

ANTHONY EVANS

Excerpt from: ***America: Turning a Nation to God***
Copyright © 2015 by Anthony T. Evans
Publisher: Moody Publishers
www.moodypublishers.com
ISBN: 978-0-8024-1267-6
Default Bible translation: NASB

About the Author:

Tony Evans is one of the most respected leaders in evangelical circles. As a well-known pastor, teacher, author, and speaker, he has devoted his life and ministry to presenting biblical truth and its uncompromising application to the whole of life. Dr. Evans' innate ability to connect biblical principles to everyday realities continues to transform lives all over the world. He has written numerous books and booklets, including *Oneness Embraced*, *The Kingdom Agenda*, *Raising Kingdom Kids*, and *Kingdom Man*. For more information, visit: www.ocbfchurch.org.

DAVID FERGUSON

Original article by David Ferguson and the Great Commandment Network: **"It's Our Calling"**
Excerpts also from: ***Relational Foundations***
Excerpts also from: ***Relational Discipleship***
Contact David at: info@greatcommandment.net

About the Author:

David Ferguson serves as the Executive Director for the Great Commandment Network, which serves more than twenty denominations and para-church ministries through pastoral care, training strategies, and resource development. David is a member of the Oxford Society of Scholars and has authored more than twenty-five books, including *Relational Foundations, Relational Discipleship, Intimate Encounters,* and *The Great Commandment Principle*. David and his wife Teresa are the co-founders of Intimate Life Ministries and the Center for Relational Leadership and have conducted training and coaching events for ministers and leaders from more than 50 countries.

RONNIE FLOYD

Excerpt from: **"Love One Another" by Ronnie Floyd**
Issue 37 of *Prayer Connect*
Copyright © Church Prayer Leaders Network

About the Author:

Ronnie Floyd was elected as president and CEO of the Executive Committee of the Southern Baptist Convention on April 2, 2019. Floyd's proudest accomplishments stem from his personal life. He and his wife, Jeana, have been married for 42 years. They have two sons, Josh and Nick. Follow him on Twitter @RonnieFloyd or www.RonnieFloyd.com.

DENNIS GALLAHER

Excerpt from e-book: *A Sabbath Rest*
www.amazon.com/dp/B008RLYFL4

About the Author:

Dennis Gallaher has been caring for God's people for forty-one years, the past thirty years at Freedom Fellowship Church. Dennis has a degree in Ministry from Hill Country Bible College, a BA in Biblical Counseling from Trinity College, and a MA in Professional Counseling from Texas State University. In his heart of hearts, he is committed to shepherding God's people and loving his church with sincerity and dedication. Read Dennis' blogs at www.dennisgallaher.com.

ALTON GARRISON

Excerpt from: *A Spirit-Empowered Church: An Acts 2 Ministry Model*
Copyright © 2015
Publisher: Influence Resources
ISBN: 978-1-6815-4001-6

About the Author:

Alton Garrison serves as the Assistant General Superintendent of the Assemblies of God. In addition, he serves as the director of the Acts 2 Revitalization Initiative, which helps churches renew their spiritual vitality and reach their full kingdom potential. He is the author of *Hope in America's Crisis*, *Building the Winning Team*, *The Acts 2 Church*, and *The 360° Disciple*. Garrison and his wife Johanna currently reside in Springfield, MO. To purchase the full resource, go to amazon.com.

TIM KIMMEL

Excerpt from: *Grace-Filled Marriage: The Missing Piece: The Place to Start* by Dr. Tim Kimmel
Copyright © 2013, 2015 Tim Kimmel
Reprinted by permission of Worthy Books, an imprint of Hachette Book Group, Inc.
ISBN: 978-1-6179-5483-2

About the Author:

Tim Kimmel is the founder and Executive Director of Family Matters, whose goal is to see families transformed by God's grace into instruments of reformation and restoration.

Tim develops resources for families and churches, and conducts conferences across the country on the unique pressures that confront today's families. Not only is Tim a well-known speaker, he has authored many books including *Grace Based Parenting* and, most recently, *Connecting Church and Home* and *Grace Filled Marriage*. Tim and Darcy count their role as parents and grandparents as one of their greatest joys. God has blessed them with four children, their spouses, and a growing flock of grandkids. Go to familymatters.net for the full resource.

CAROLINE LEAF

Excerpt from: *Switch On Your Brain* by Caroline Leaf
Copyright © 2013 Dr. Caroline Leaf
Used by permission of Baker Books, a division of Baker Publishing Group
ISBN: 978-0-8010-1624-0

About the Author:

Caroline Leaf is a communication pathologist and audiologist who has worked in the area of cognitive neuroscience since 1995. Her pioneering work in neuroplasticity—showing that changes in thinking actually change the brain and can effect behavioral change—paved the way for her current research on how scientific principles are supported by Scripture and vice versa. She has been featured *on Enjoying Everyday Life* with Joyce Meyer, *LIFE Today* with James and Betty Robison, *Today* with Marilyn and Sarah, and *It's Supernatural* with Sid Roth, and *Doctor to Doctor*. To purchase the full resource, go to amazon.com.

JADE LEE

Excerpt from: *The Ferguson Dilemma: Healing America's Racial Wounds*
Copyright © 2017 Jade Lee
Publisher: International Publishing Inc., 2017
ISBN: 978-1-9469-1702-7

About the Author:

Jade Lee—a native of Deptford, NJ—was a 2001 Junior All American, an eleven-time record holder, a six-time MEAC Conference Team Champion, and an Indoor Championship MVP during her tenure as a Hampton University collegiate athlete. Throughout these years, she also developed a passion for ministry and a desire to share the gospel of Jesus Christ, deciding to leave her track aspirations for ministerial work. Jade now speaks at local schools and churches and travels internationally to preach the gospel and share the message of racial reconciliation with her husband, Pastor Corey Lee. For more about this resource, go to thefergusondilemma.com.

JOSH MCDOWELL

Excerpt from: *10 Ways to Say "I Love You"*
Copyright © 2015 by Josh McDowell Ministry. All rights reserved.
Publisher: Harvest House Publishers
Eugene, Oregon 97402
www.harvesthousepublishers.com
Used by permission
ISBN: 978-0-7369-5387-0
To order the complete book, go to www.josh.org.
Excerpt from: *God Breathed: The Undeniable Power and Reliability of Scripture*
Copyright © 2015 Josh McDowell Ministry
Publisher: Tyndale House Publishers, Inc.
ISBN: 978-1-6305-8941-7

About the Author:

Josh McDowell has been reaching the spiritually skeptical for more than five decades. Since beginning ministry in 1961, Josh has spoken to more than 25 million people in 128 countries. He is the author or coauthor of 148 books (with over 51 million copies distributed worldwide), including *Straight Talk with Your Kids about Sex*, *Experience Your Bible*, *Evidence for the Historical Jesus*, *More Than a Carpenter* (over 15 million copies printed in eighty-five languages), and *The New Evidence That Demands a Verdict* (recognized by *World* magazine as one of the twentieth century's top forty books). Josh continues to travel throughout the United States and to various countries around the world, helping young people and adults strengthen their faith and understanding of Scripture. Josh and his wife, Dottie, have been married for over 40 years and have four children and numerous grandchildren.

KEVIN PALAU

Excerpt from: *Unlikely: Setting Aside Our Differences to Live Out the Gospel* by Kevin Palau
Copyright © 2015 by Kevin Palau
Publisher: Howard Books – A Division of Simon and Schuster, Inc.
ISBN: 978-1-4767-8944-6

About the Author:

Kevin Palau is the son of international evangelist Luis Palau. He joined the Luis Palau Association in 1985 and began directing the day-to-day operation of the ministry in the late 1990s. Under his leadership, LPA has produced some of the largest Christian events ever staged, created a world-wide network of hundreds of partner evangelists, and developed new models for citywide outreach that integrate major community service initiatives with open-air evangelistic gatherings. Kevin holds a degree in religious studies from Wheaton College and lives in Beaverton, Oregon with his wife, Michelle. They have three adult children.

LES PARROTT

Excerpts from: *Love Like That*
Copyright © Les Parrott
Publisher: Nelson Books—an imprint of Thomas Nelson
ISBN: 978-1-4002-0781-7

About the Author:

Les Parrott, PhD, is a psychologist and #1 New York Times bestselling author. He and his wife, Dr. Leslie Parrott, are cofounders of the game-changing "Better Love Assessment" (see BetterLove. com). Dr. Parrott's books have sold over 3 million copies in more than two dozen languages and include the award-winning Saving Your Marriage Before It Starts. Dr. Les Parrott has been featured in US Today and the New York Times. He's appeared on CNN, Fox News, Good Morning America, The Today Show, The View, and Oprah. Visit LesandLeslie.com and LoveLikeThatBook.com.

DENNIS RAINEY

Excerpt from: *The Forgotten Commandment*, originally published as *The Tribute and The Promise*
Copyright © Dennis Rainey, 1994
Publisher: FamilyLife® Publishing (April 2014)
To buy the complete book, go to www.shop.familylife.com.

About the Author:

Dennis Rainey is the president and CEO of FamilyLife, a subsidiary of Cru. Since the organization began in 1976, Dennis' leadership has enabled FamilyLife to grow into a dynamic and vital ministry that offers families blueprints for living godly lives. Dennis has authored or co-authored more than two dozen books including the best-selling *Moments Together for Couples* and *Staying Close*. Dennis and Barbara have been married since 1972 and love laughing together with their six children and numerous grandchildren. For more information, go to www.familylife.com.

JAMIE RASMUSSEN

Excerpt from: *How Joyful People Think*
Copyright © 2018 Jamie Rasmussen
Publisher: Baker Books
ISBN: 978-0-8010-7575-9

About the Author:

Jamie Rasmussen is the senior pastor of Scottsdale Bible Church, which has been regularly listed on *Outreach Magazine*'s Top 100 list in both size and speed of growth for the past ten years. He has been an ordained pastor for more than twenty-five years and has served growing churches in Detroit, Michigan; London, Ontario (Canada); and Cleveland, Ohio. He lives in Arizona. Go to amazon.com to purchase the full resource.

SAMUEL RODRIGUEZ

Excerpt from: *The Lamb's Agenda: Why Jesus Is Calling You to a Life of Righteousness and Justice*
Copyright © 2013 by Samuel Rodriguez
Publisher: Thomas Nelson
ISBN: 978-1-4002-0449-6
Default Bible translation: NIV

About the Author:

Samuel Rodriguez is President of the National Hispanic Christian Leadership Conference—America's largest Hispanic Christian organization. Named by *CNN* as "The leader of the Hispanic Evangelical Movement" and by the *San Francisco Chronicle* as one of America's new evangelical leaders, Rodriguez is also the recipient of the Martin Luther King Jr. Award presented by the Congress on Racial Equality. A featured speaker in White House and congressional meetings, he has been featured, profiled, and quoted by such media outlets as *The New York Times*, *Christianity Today*, the *Washington Post*, the *Wall Street Journal*, *Newsweek*, *Univision*, *Fox News*, *Time*, and *Ministries Today*. Rodriguez is also the Senior Pastor of New Season Christian Worship Center in Sacramento, CA.

DAVE RUNYON

Excerpt from: ***The Art of Neighboring*** by Jay Pathak and Dave Runyon
Copyright © 2012 Jay Pathak and David Runyon
Used by permission of Baker Books, a division of Baker Publishing Group
ISBN: 978-0-8010-1459-8

About the Author:

Dave Runyon helps faith, business, and government leaders unite around common causes in the Denver metro area. He serves as the Executive Director of CityUnite, and serves as a consultant for businesses who have a desire to give back in their communities. Previously, Dave was a pastor at Foothills Community Church and The Next Level Church. In 2010, he launched a neighboring movement that has now spread to over fifteen hundred churches around the country. He speaks locally and nationally, encouraging leaders to work together for the good of their cities. Dave and his wife, Lauren, have four kids.

TERRI SNEAD

Excerpt from: ***Parenting with Intimacy***
Copyright © David & Teresa Ferguson, Paul & Vicky Warren, and Terri Snead
Publisher: Relationship Press, 1995
ISBN: 1 56476 522

Excerpt from: ***Extreme Home Makeover***
Copyright © 2010 Relationship Press
Publisher: Relationship Press, 2010
ISBN: 1893307573

About the Author:

Terri Snead is a teacher, conference speaker, and professional counselor. She leads the Training and Resources Division of the Great Commandment Network, where she has co-authored numerous books with her father, Dr. David Ferguson. Terri is married to Wayne, with whom she enjoys lots of time with their four kids and two grandkids. To order GCN's resources, go to www.greatcommandment.net

ED STETZER AND PHILIP NATION

Excerpt from *Compelled by Love* by Ed Stetzer and Philip Nation
Copyright © 2008 by Ed Stetzer and Philip Nation
Reprinted as *Compelled*,© 2012 by Ed Stetzer and Philip Nation. Published by New Hope Publishers.
All rights reserved. Used by permission.
ISBN: 978-1-5966-9351-7

About the Authors:

Ed Stetzer has planted, revitalized, and pastored churches. He has trained pastors and church planters on five continents; holds two masters degrees and two doctorates; and has written dozens of articles and books. Ed is a contributing editor for *Christianity Today*, a columnist for *Outreach Magazine* and *Catalyst Monthly*, serves on the advisory council of Sermon Central and *Christianity Today*'s Building Church Leaders, and is frequently cited or interviewed in news outlets such as *USA Today* and *CNN*. His primary role is as vice president of Research and Ministry Development for LifeWay Christian Resources.

Philip Nation works as the Director of Adult Ministry Publishing at LifeWay Christian Resources and serves as the teaching pastor for The Fellowship, a multi-site church in Nashville, TN. He earned a Doctor of Ministry from Southeastern Baptist Theological Seminary. His books include *Compelled: Living the Mission of God* and *Transformational Discipleship: How People Really Grow*. He is the happy husband of Angie and a father to Andrew and Chris.

JOHN TRENT

Excerpt from: *The Language of Love: The Secret to Being Instantly Understood* by Gary Smalley and John Trent
Copyright © 1988, 1991, 2006, 2018 John Trent, Ph.D. and Gary Smalley
Publisher: Tyndale House Publishers, Inc.
ISBN: 978-1-5899-7683-2

About the Author:

John Trent is an award-winning, best-selling author and speaker. He has published more than twenty books, including *The Blessing*, which has over two million copies in print. Dr. Trent has been a sought-after keynote speaker, and has appeared on numerous radio and television programs, including *The Oprah Winfrey Show*. He currently lives in Arizona where he runs StrongFamilies—a nonprofit dedicated to helping others find joy, restoration, and connection in their most valuable relationships. To purchase the full resource, go to strongfamilies.com.

STEVE UHLMANN

Original article by Steve Uhlmann: **"God IS Love"**

About the Author:

Steve and Barbara Uhlmann have actively supported marriage and family ministries together for the last forty years. As a successful CEO of an international plastics company, Steve has known business success, but continues to see relationships as the way to reveal Jesus to the people around us. Steve and Barbara have dedicated themselves to sharing the principles of love and change that transformed their own lives. For more information, you can contact Steve at familyoffices.org.

DALLAS WILLARD

Excerpt from: *The Great Omission* by Dallas Willard
Copyright © 2006 by Dallas Willard
Reprinted by permission of HarperCollins Publishers
ISBN: 978-0-0608-8243-3
Default Bible translation: NIV

About the Author:

Dallas Willard was a professor in the School of Philosophy at the University of Southern California in Los Angeles. He was Director of the School of Philosophy and taught at the University of Wisconsin. Dallas also lectured and published significant works on the topic of religion. *The Great Omission* received a *Christianity Today* Annual Book Award in the Christian Living category in 2007. Another of Dallas' books, *The Divine Conspiracy*, was released in 1998 and was selected as *Christianity Today's* "Book of the Year" for 1999.

APPENDIX 1

ABOUT THE GREAT COMMANDMENT NETWORK

The Great Commandment Network is an international collaborative network of strategic kingdom leaders from the faith community, marketplace, education, and caregiving fields who prioritize the powerful simplicity of the words of Jesus to love God, love others, and see others become His followers (Matthew 22:37–40, Matthew 28:19–20).

The Great Commandment Network is served through the following:

Relationship Press – This team collaborates, supports, and joins together with churches, denominational partners, and professional associates to develop, print, and produce resources that facilitate ongoing Great Commandment ministry.

The Center for Relational Leadership – Their mission is to teach, train, and mentor both ministry and corporate leaders in Great Commandment principles, seeking to equip leaders with relational skills so they might lead as Jesus led.

The Galatians 6:6 Retreat Ministry – This ministry offers a unique two-day retreat for ministers and their spouses for personal renewal and for reestablishing and affirming ministry and family priorities.

The Center for Relational Care (CRC) – The CRC provides therapy and support to relationships in crisis through an accelerated process of growth and healing, including Relational Care Intensives for couples, families, and singles.

For more information on how you, your church, ministry, denomination, or movement can be served by the Great Commandment Network write or call:

Great Commandment Network
2511 South Lakeline Blvd.
Cedar Park, Texas 78613
#800-881-8008

Or visit our website: GreatCommandment.net

APPENDIX 2

A SPIRIT-EMPOWERED FAITH

Expresses Itself in Great Commission Living Empowered by Great Commandment Love

 begins with the end in mind: The Great Commission calls us to make disciples.

"Go therefore and make disciples of all the nations, baptizing them in the name of the Father and the Son and the Holy Spirit teaching them to observe all things that I have commanded you; and lo, I am with you always, even to the end of the age" (Matthew 28:19–20).

The ultimate goal of our faith journey is to relate to the person of Jesus, because it is our relational connection to Jesus that will produce Christlikeness and spiritual growth. This relational perspective of discipleship is required if we hope to have a faith that is marked by the Spirit's power.

Models of discipleship that are based solely upon what we know and what we do are incomplete, lacking the empowerment of a life of loving and living intimately with Jesus. A Spirit-empowered faith is relational and impossible to realize apart from a special work of the Spirit. For exam- ple, the Spirit-empowered outcome of "listening to and hearing God" implies relationship—it is both relational in focus and requires the Holy Spirit's power to live.

 begins at the right place: The Great Commandment calls us to start with loving God and loving others.

"'You shall love the Lord your God with all your heart, with all your soul, and with all your mind.' This is the first and great commandment. And the second is like it: 'You shall love your neighbor as yourself.' On these two commandments hang all the Law and the Prophets" (Matthew 22:37–40).

Relevant discipleship does not begin with doctrines or teaching, parables or stewardship—but with loving the Lord with all your heart, mind, soul, and strength and then loving the people closest to you. Since Matthew 22:37–40 gives us the first and greatest commandment, a Spirit-empowered faith starts where the Great Commandment tells us to start: A disciple must first learn to deeply love the Lord and to express His love to the "nearest ones"—his or her family, church, and community (and in that order).

 **embraces a relational process of Christlikeness.**

"Walk while you have the light, lest darkness overtake you" (John 12:35).

Scripture reminds us that there are three sources of light for our journey: Jesus, His Word, and His people. The process of discipleship (or becoming more like Jesus) occurs as we relate intimately with each source of light.

Spirit-empowered discipleship will require a lifestyle of:

- Fresh encounters with Jesus (John 8:12)

- Frequent experiences of Scripture (Psalm 119:105)

- Faithful engagement with God's people (Matthew 5:14)

 can be defined with observable outcomes using a biblical framework.

"And He Himself gave some to be apostles, some prophets, some evangelists, and some pastors and teachers,for the equipping of the saints for the work of ministry, for the edifying of the body of Christ" (Ephesians 4:11–12).

The metrics for measuring Spirit-empowered faith or the growth of a disciple come from Scripture and are organized/framed around four distinct dimensions of a disciple who serves.

A relational framework for organizing Spirit-Empowered Discipleship Out- comes draws from a cluster analysis of several Greek (diakoneo, leitourgeo, dou- leuo) and Hebrew words ('abad, Sharat), which elaborate on the Ephesians 4:12 declaration that Christ's followers are to be equipped for works of ministry or service. Therefore, the 40 Spirit Empowered Faith Outcomes have been identified and organized around:

- Serving/loving the Lord – While they were ministering to the Lord and fasting (Acts 13:2 NASB).[1]

- Serving/loving the Word – But we will devote ourselves to prayer and to theministry of the word (Acts 6:4 NASB).[2]

- Serving/loving people – Through love serve one another (Galatians 5:13 NASB).[3]

- Serving/loving His mission – Now all these things are from God, who reconciled us to Himself through Christ and gave us the ministry of reconciliation (2 Corinthians 5:18 NASB).[4]

1   Ferguson, David L. Great Commandment Principle. Cedar Park, Texas: Relationship Press, 2013.
2   Ferguson, David L. Relational Foundations. Cedar Park, Texas: Relationship Press, 2004.
3   Ferguson, David L. Relational Discipleship. Cedar Park, Texas: Relationship Press, 2005.
4   "Spirit Empowered Outcomes," www.empowered21.com, Empowered 21 Global
    Council, http://empowered21.com/discipleship-materials/.

APPENDIX 3

A SPIRIT-EMPOWERED DISCIPLE LOVES THE LORD THROUGH

L1. **Practicing thanksgiving in all things**
"Enter the gates with thanksgiving" (Ps. 100:4). "In everything give thanks" (I Th. 5:18). "As sorrowful, yet always rejoicing" (II Cor. 6:10).

L2. **Listening to and hearing God for direction and discernment**
"Speak Lord, Your servant is listening" (I Sam. 3:8–9). "Mary…listening to the Lord's word, seated at his feet" (Lk.10:38–42). "Shall I not share with Abraham what I am about to do?" (Gen. 18:17). "His anointing teaches you all things" (I Jn. 2:27).

L3. **Experiencing God as He really is through deepened intimacy with Him**
"Hear, O Israel: The Lord our God, the Lord is one. Love the Lord your God with all your heart and with all your soul and with all your strength" (Deut. 6:4,5). "Yet the Lord longs to be gracious to you; therefore he will rise up to show you compassion. For the Lord is a God of justice" (Is. 30:18). See also John 14:9.

L4. **Rejoicing regularly in my identity as "His Beloved"**
"And His banner over me is love" (Song of Sol. 2:4). "To the praise of the glory of His grace, which He freely bestowed on us in the beloved" (Eph. 1:6). "For the Lord gives to His beloved even in their sleep" (Ps. 127:2).

L5. **Living with a passionate longing for purity and to please Him in all things**
"Who may ascend the hill of the Lord—he who has clean hands and a pure heart" (Ps. 24:3). "Beloved, let us cleanse ourselves from all of flesh and spirit, perfecting holiness in the fear of God" (II Cor. 7:1). "I always do the things that are pleasing to Him" (Jn. 8:29). "Though He slay me, yet will I hope in Him" (Job 13:15).

L6. **Consistent practice of self-denial, fasting, and solitude rest**
"He turned and said to Peter, '"Get behind me, Satan! You are an obstacle to me. You are thinking not as God does, but as human beings do'" (Matt. 16:23). "But you when you fast…" (Mt. 6:17). "Be still and know that I am God" (Ps. 46:10).

L7. **Entering often into Spirit-led praise and worship**
"Bless the Lord O my soul and all that is within me…" (Ps. 103:1). "Worship the Lord with reverence" (Ps. 2:11). "I praise Thee O Father, Lord of heaven and earth…" (Mt. 11:25).

L8. **Disciplined, bold and believing prayer**
"Pray at all times in the Spirit" (Eph. 6:18). "Call unto me and I will answer…" (Jer. 33:3)). "If you ask according to His will—He hears—and you will have…" (I Jn. 5: 14–15).

L9. **Yielding to the Spirit's fullness as life in the Spirit brings supernatural intimacy with the Lord, manifestation of divine gifts, and witness of the fruit of the Spirit**
"For by one Spirit we were all baptized into one body, whether Jews or Greeks, whether slaves or free, and we were all made to drink of one Spirit" (I Cor. 12:13). "You shall receive power when the Holy Spirit comes upon you" (Acts 1:8). "But to each one is given the manifestation of the Spirit for the common good" (I Cor. 12:7). See also, I Pet. 4:10, and Rom. 12:6.

L10. **Practicing the presence of the Lord, yielding to the Spirit's work of Christlikeness**
"And we who with unveiled faces all reflect the Lord's glory, are being transformed into His likeness from glory to glory which comes from the Lord, who is the Spirit"
(II Cor. 3:18). "As the deer pants after the water brooks, so my soul pants after You, O God" (Ps. 42:1).

A SPIRIT-EMPOWERED DISCIPLE
LIVES THE WORD THROUGH

W1. **Frequently being led by the Spirit into deeper love for the One who wrote the Word**
"Love the Lord thy God—love thy neighbor; upon these two commandments deepens all the law and prophets" (Mt. 22:37-40). "I delight in Your commands because I love them." (Ps. 119:47). "The ordinances of the Lord are pure—they are more precious than gold—sweeter than honey" (Ps. 19:9-10).

W2. **Being a "living epistle" in reverence and awe as His Word becomes real in my life, vocation, and calling**
"You yourselves are our letter—known and read by all men" (II Cor. 3:2). "And the Word became flesh and dwelt among us" (Jn. 1:14). "Husbands love your wives—cleansing her by the washing with water through the Word" (Eph. 5:26). See also Tit. 2:5. "Whatever you do, do your work heartily, as for the Lord..." (Col. 3:23).

W3. **Yielding to the scripture's protective cautions and transforming power to bring life change in me**
"I gain understanding from Your precepts; therefore I hate every wrong path" (Ps. 119:104). "Be it done unto me according to Your word" (Lk. 1:38). "How can a young man keep his way pure? By living according to Your word" (Ps. 119:9). See also Col. 3:16–17.

W4. **Humbly and vulnerably sharing of the Spirit's transforming work through the Word**
"I will speak of your statutes before kings and will not be put to shame" (Ps. 119:46). "Preach the word; be ready in season and out to shame" (II Tim. 4:2).

W5. **Meditating consistently on more and more of the Word hidden in the heart**
"I have hidden Your Word in my heart that I might not sin against You" (Ps. 119:12). "May the words of my mouth and the meditation of my heart be pleasing in Your sight, O Lord, my rock and my redeemer" (Ps. 19:14).

W6. **Encountering Jesus in the Word for deepened transformation in Christlikeness**
"All of us, gazing with unveiled face on the glory of the Lord, are being transformed into the same image from glory to glory, as from the Lord who is the Spirit" (II Cor. 3:18). "If you abide in Me and My words abide in you, ask whatever you wish, and it will be done for you" (Jn. 15:7). See also Lk. 24:32, Ps. 119:136, and II Cor. 1:20.

W7. **A life-explained as one of "experiencing scripture"**
"This is that spoken of by the prophets" (Acts 2:16). "My comfort in my suffering is this: Your promise preserves my life" (Ps. 119:50). "My soul is consumed with longing for Your laws at all times" (Ps. 119:20).

W8. **Living "naturally supernatural", in all of life, as His Spirit makes the written Word *(logos)* the living Word *(Rhema)***
"Faith comes by hearing and hearing by the Word (Rhema) of Christ" (Rom. 10:17). "Your Word is a lamp to my feet and a light for my path" (Ps. 119:105).

W9. **Living abundantly "in the present" as His Word brings healing to hurt and anger, guilt, fear and condemnation— which are *heart hindrances* to life abundant**
"The thief comes to steal, kill and destroy..." (John 10:10). "I run in the path of Your commands for You have set my heart free" (Ps. 119:32). "...and you shall know the truth and the truth shall set you free" (Jn. 8:32). "For freedom Christ set us free; so stand firm and do not submit again to the yoke of slavery" (Gal. 5:1).

W10. **Implicit, unwavering trust that His Word will never fail**
"The grass withers and the flower fades but the Word of God abides forever" (Is. 40:8). "So will My word be which goes forth from My mouth, it will not return to me empty" (Is. 55:11).

A SPIRIT-EMPOWERED DISCIPLE
LOVES PEOPLE THROUGH

P1. Living a Spirit-led life of doing good in all of life: relationships and vocation, community and calling
"…He went about doing good…" (Acts 10:38). "Let your light shine before men in such a way that they may see your good works, and glorify your Father who is in heaven" (Mt. 5:16). "But love your enemies, and do good, and lend, expecting nothing in return, and your reward will be great, and you will be sons of the Most High; for He Himself is kind to ungrateful and evil men" (Lk. 6:35). See also Rom. 15:2.

P2. Startling people with loving initiatives to give *first*
"Give, and it will be given to you. They will pour into your lap a good measure—pressed down, shaken together, and running over. For by your standard of measure it will be measured to you in return" (Lk. 6:38). "But Jesus was saying, 'Father, forgive them; for they do not know what they are doing.' (Lk. 23:34). See also Lk. 23:43 and Jn. 19:27.

P3. Discerning the relational needs of others with a heart to give of His love
"Let no unwholesome word proceed from your mouth, but only such a word as is good for edification according to the need of the moment, so that it will give grace to those who hear" (Eph. 4:29). "And my God will supply all your needs according to His riches in glory in Christ Jesus" (Phil. 4:19). See also Lk. 6:30.

P4. Seeing people as needing BOTH redemption from sin AND intimacy in relationships, addressing both human fallen-ness and aloneness
"But God demonstrates His own love toward us, in that while we were yet sinners, Christ died for us" (Rom. 5:8). "When Jesus came to the place, He looked up and said to him, 'Zaccheus, hurry and come down, for today I must stay at your house'" (Lk. 19:5). See also Mk. 8:24 and Gen. 2:18.

P5. Ministering His life and love to our *nearest ones* at home and with family as well as faithful engagement in His Body, the church
"You husbands in the same way, live with your wives in an understanding way, as with someone weaker, since she is a woman; and show her honor as a fellow heir of the grace of life, so that your prayers will not be hindered" (I Pet. 3:7). See also I Pet. 3:1 and Ps. 127:3.

P6. Expressing the fruit of the Spirit as a lifestyle and identity
"But the fruit of the Spirit is love, joy, peace, patience, kindness, goodness, faithfulness, gentleness, self-control…" (Gal. 5:22-23). "With the fruit of a man's mouth his stomach will be satisfied; He will be satisfied with the product of his lips" (Prov. 18:20).

P7. Expecting and demonstrating the supernatural as His spiritual gifts are made manifest and His grace is at work by His Spirit
*"In the power of signs and wonders, in the power of the **Spirit**; so that from Jerusalem and round about as far as Illyricum I have fully preached the gospel of Christ" (Rom. 15:19). "Truly, truly, I say to you, he who believes in Me, the works that I do, he will do also…"(Jn. 14:12). See also I Cor. 14:1.*

P8. Taking courageous initiative as a peacemaker, reconciling relationships along life's journey
"…Live in peace with one another" (I Th. 5:13). "For He Himself is our peace, who made both groups into one and broke down the barrier of the dividing wall" (Eph. 2:14). "Therefore, confess your sins to one another, and pray for one another so that you may be healed. See also Jas. 5:16 and Eph. 4:31–32.

P9. Demonstrating His love to an ever growing network of "others" as He continues to challenge us to love "beyond our comfort"
"The one who says, 'I have come to know Him,' and does not keep His commandments, is a liar, and the truth is not in him" (I Jn. 2:4). "If someone says, 'I love God,' and hates his brother, he is a liar; for the one who does not love his brother whom he has seen, cannot love God whom he has not seen" (I Jn. 4:20).

P10. Humbly acknowledging to the Lord, ourselves, and others that it is Jesus in and through us who is loving others at their point of need
"Take My yoke upon you and learn from Me, for I am gentle and humble in heart, and you will find rest for your souls" (Mt. 11:29). "If I then, the Lord and the Teacher, washed your feet, you also ought to wash one another's feet" (Jn. 13:14).

A SPIRIT-EMPOWERED DISCIPLE
LIVES HIS MISSION THROUGH

M1. Imparting the gospel and one's very life in daily activities and relationships, vocation and community
"Having so fond an affection for you, we were well-pleased to impart to you not only the gospel of God but also our own lives, because you had become very dear to us" (I Th. 2:8-9). See also Eph. 6:19.

M2. Expressing and extending the Kingdom of God as compassion, justice, love, and forgiveness are shared
"I must preach the kingdom of God to the other cities also, for I was sent for this purpose'" (Lk. 4:43). "As You sent Me into the world, I also have sent them into the world"(Jn. 17:18). "Restore to me the joy of Your salvation and sustain me with a willing spirit. Then I will teach transgressors Your ways, and sinners will be converted to you"(Ps. 51:12–13). See also Mic. 6:8.

M3. Championing Jesus as the only hope of eternal life and abundant living
"There is no salvation through anyone else, nor is there any other name under heaven given to the human race by which we are to be saved" (Acts 4:12). "A thief comes only to steal and slaughter and destroy; I came so that they might have life and have it more abundantly" (Jn. 10:10). See also Acts 4:12, Jn. 10:10, and Jn. 14:6.

M4. Yielding to the Spirit's role to convict others as He chooses, resisting expressions of condemnation
"And He, when He comes, will convict the world concerning sin and righteousness and judgment…"(Jn. 16:8). "Who is the one who condemns? Christ Jesus is He who died, yes, rather who was raised, who is at the right hand of God, who also intercedes for us" (Rom. 8:34). See also Rom. 8:1.

M5. Ministering His life and love to the "least of these"
"Then He will answer them, 'Truly I say to you, to the extent that you did not do it to one of the least of these, you did not do it to Me'" (Mt. 25:45). "Pure and undefiled religion in the sight of our God and Father is this: to visit orphans and widows in their distress, and to keep oneself unstained by the world" (Jas. 1:27).

M6. Bearing witness of a confident peace and expectant hope in God's Lordship in all things
"Now may the Lord of peace Himself continually grant you peace in every circumstance. The Lord be with you all!" (II Thess. 3:16). "Let the peace of Christ rule in your hearts, to which indeed you were called in one body; and be thankful" (Col. 3:15). See also Rom. 8:28 and Ps. 146:5.

M7. Faithfully sharing of time, talent, gifts, and resources in furthering His mission
"Of this church I was made a minister according to the stewardship from God bestowed on me for your benefit, so that I might fully carry out the preaching of the word of God" (Col. 1:25). "From everyone who has been given much, much will be required; and to whom they entrusted much, of him they will ask all the more" (Lk. 12:48). See also I Cor. 4:1–2.

M8. Attentive listening to others' *story*, vulnerably sharing of our story, and a sensitive witness of Jesus' story as life's ultimate hope; developing your story of prodigal, pre-occupied and pain-filled living; listening for other's story and sharing Jesus' story
"…but sanctify Christ as Lord in your hearts, always being ready to make a defense to everyone who asks you to give an account for the hope that is in you, yet with gentleness and reverence" (I Pet. 3:15). "…because this son of mine was dead, and has come to life again" (Luke 11:24). (Mark 5:21–42). (Jn. 9:1–35).

M9. Pouring our life into others, making disciples who in turn make disciples of others
"Go therefore and make disciples of all nations, baptizing them in the name of the Father and the Son and the Holy Spirit, teaching them to observe all that I commanded you; and lo, I am with you always, even to the end of the age" (Mt. 28:19–20). See also II Tim. 2:2.

M10. Living submissively within His Body, the Church as instruction and encouragement, reproof and correction are graciously received by faithful disciples
"…and be subject to one another in the fear of Christ" (Eph. 5:21). "Brethren, even if anyone is caught in any trespass, you who are spiritual, restore such a one in a spirit of gentleness; each one looking to yourself, so that you too will not be tempted" (Gal. 6:1). See also Gal. 6:2.

Engage with the Called 2 Love Movement:

- **In your family . . .** as loving your nearest ones becomes a top priority in imparting faith, to next generations.

- **In your church . . .** as a mentor couple, small group leader, or workshop presenter, living out Christ's new Commandment to love one another and help others to do the same (John 13:34).

- **In your community . . .** as being Called2Love like Jesus transforms families, neighborhoods, schools, and the marketplace.

- **As a church . . .** where the powerful simplicity of Great Commission Living Empowered by Great Commandment Love takes any church to the next level of Kingdom impact (Matthew 28:19-20, 22:37-40).

Visit *GreatCommandment.net* **to find out more!**

More Called 2 Love Resources

Order at: **GreatCommandment.net/resources**

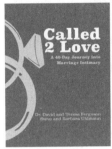

Called 2 Love
A 40-Day Journey into Marriage Intimacy

Using the power of story, the authors lead couples along their own journey to better know and care for each other. An excellent resource for couple mentoring, small groups and premarital counseling.

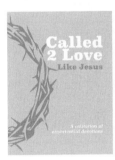

Called 2 Love
A 40-Day Journey in Loving Like Jesus

An anthology of teachings and practical exercises from notable followers of Jesus.

Explore the transforming power of your call to love, "*as you have been loved.*" Also included are practical disciplines to deepen your love of the Lord followed by loving family, friends, and those who need Jesus.

Called 2 Love
The Uhlmann Story

One couple's journey from a mere existence to deepened marriage intimacy.

Married for more than 50 years, Steve and Barbara continue to see relationships as the way to reveal Jesus to the people around us. In their new book, *Called2Love: The Uhlmann Story*, they share the principles of love and change that transformed their lives.

NOTES

NOTES

NOTES

NOTES

NOTES